THE CURRENT FIGHT WITHIN

THE CURRENT FIGHT WITHIN

The Effects Terrorism Has on People, Policy, Emergency First Responders, and Military Service Members

Edward P. Ackley, 1stSgt USMC Retired

authorHOUSE®

AuthorHouse™
1663 Liberty Drive
Bloomington, IN 47403
www.authorhouse.com
Phone: 1-800-839-8640

Published by AuthorHouse   08/13/2015

ISBN: 978-1-4817-0740-4 (sc)
ISBN: 978-1-4817-0739-8 (hc)
ISBN: 978-1-4817-0738-1 (e)

Library of Congress Control Number: 2013901144

Print information available on the last page.

Contents

PREFACE

The initial thought to write a book came from constantly hearing people discussing homeland security concerns and blaming the United States government for not working proactively on terrorism issues. To the contrary, readers will gain understanding that all measures for such importance are in place, but require much effort and time to see results. Each chapter starts with a question I have heard people ask.

Taking into consideration the many views that I have heard people discuss in open conversation, I analyzed the common issues presented and have attempted to write the book for all audiences. It may, however, be of special interest to members of the military and emergency services.

My research became more complex than I had anticipated, as there is so much material on each topic I include within the chapters. In the spirit of making the material approachable for readers, my opinions in the book are based purely on my research and my personal experience. There are many overlapping discussions that sum up my concern with terrorism.

The reader may experience frustration, wonder, empathy, and even mutual respect and understanding regarding emergency response to terrorism and terrorism prevention. I noticed that writing a book for a broad audience required a lot of effort not to offend or exclude any group of people. In addition, I made every effort to provide an easy understanding of the material I researched. Homeland security is such a broad field that I was only able to address some aspects.

When I was deployed to Iraq in 2003, it came very apparent that the enemy wasn't easily recognized in the typical military fighting uniform; in fact, they blended into the very communities we assisted by providing food, water, safety and security. After reading the book, you will better understand that the photo on the cover, even though it was taken in Iraq, it does explain an area of concern within the United States.

In short, I feel that my effort and results are exceptional for the purpose, and hope the book achieves more scope of our country's "Current Fight Within." I encourage the reader to conduct more research on what you read in this book and to form your own opinions. At the end of the book is my biography that discusses my experience.

A terrorist can be any person from any background for any reason!

ACKNOWLEDGMENTS

Thanks to those I directly served with in the Fire Service and the Marine Corps; specifically in the military police, antiterrorism force protection, the marine security guard program, the martial arts program, and drill instructor duty. You provided me chance, opportunity, and confidence in my current life.

For those missed by many and thought of daily, a moment of silence for people taken from the life on earth and granted new life that oversees our love for one another through spirit. Each of us has experienced life lost. Each loss is different in nature but valued by the touching memories that could never be replaced by a photo or conversation.

In addition, please take time to pray for all mankind that take risks that benefit public wellbeing, community protection, and national security. These three areas cover many occupations that require very special and unique people who strive to keep stability and longevity for all Americans.

Chapter 1

HOW IS AMERICA COMBATING TERRORISM IN THE HOMELAND AND ABROAD?

AMERICANS ARE CONCERNED for their safety and many are wondering what strategy is in place to protect our nation against terrorism. In fact there are many strategies the United States uses both on US soil and abroad and I will discuss some of them in this chapter. First readers need to have a basic understanding of what combating terrorism entails.

Terrorism acts have become more deadly through the years even as the acts have become fewer. It is the responsibility of the Federal Bureau of Investigation and all domestic law enforcement agencies to investigate attacks conducted by terrorists within the United States. Terrorist threats overseas are addressed by the Department of State. All agencies involved with counterterrorism must work together to prevent attacks or mitigate incidents in the spirit of one team, one fight! In order to achieve this, investigators must take into consideration all sources available internationally and domestically to prevent terrorist attacks and to better prepare for incidents conducted by terrorists.

There are strategies, tactics, and tools available that make up the resources available to all law enforcement agencies both domestically and abroad. Some of these resources lead to the use of military forces as deemed necessary by the president of the United States when other international counterterrorism measures have failed, but domestic counterterrorism is different. Nonetheless, it is necessary for the United States to maintain a presence overseas to perform counterterrorism operations.

Prior to the 1993 World Trade Center bombing, international terrorists primarily targeted American interests overseas (Department of Justice 2005). Many remember the attacks that took place abroad including the hostage situation in Lebanon in 1980 (Jenco 1996), the bombing of Pan Am Flight over Lockerbie, Scotland, in 1988 (Zalman 2011), the explosion that took place outside the Al-Khobar Towers in 1996 (Creamer and Seat 1998), and the bombings of the American Embassies in Dar el Salaam and Tanzania in 1998.

International terrorism brings three concerns to the counterterrorism network: first, sponsored attacks; second, terrorist organizations; and finally, groups that have no affiliation to terrorist organizations but perform attacks independently (Department of Justice 2005). The Department of State is the primary agency for counterterrorism overseas (DoD Antiterrorism 2007). The Department of State has many American missions overseas. The missions are embassies, consulates, and legations, not including military bases that are also threatened by terrorism. The United States must conduct State Department counterterrorism missions in countries that condone acts of terrorism. There are countries that believe terrorism is a tool for foreign policy. These locations are also safe havens that provide protection for terrorist groups or political parties. Some of the most well known terrorist groups or political parties include Hezbollah, Al-Gama'a Al-Islamiyya, and Hamas. These organizations pose the most threat to American interests. These organizations also have their own infrastructures that allow them to plan and execute attacks overseas. Moreover, these organizations also operate in the United States through criminal activity (Department of Homeland Security 2004). The same runs true with loosely affiliated radical extremists. Loosely affiliated groups are the most dangerous, in my opinion, since they want recognition from terrorist organizations and achieve their target objective. Groups like this are similar to the group that bombed the World Trade Center in 1993 (Department of Justice 2005) because they easily conduct criminal activity in the United States. Loosely affiliated terrorist groups are unknown to law enforcement agencies. This provides much opportunity for terrorists to conduct recruiting, to harbor fugitives that hate America, and to freely train for and plan attacks.

Loosely affiliated terrorist groups are not the only threat to the United States. American far left and far right wing extremist groups and some special interest groups may also be considered as domestic terrorists (Masters 2011). These groups operate without foreign influence, and they usually target the federal government or individual citizens who they consider affiliated with the government. What makes both domestic terrorism and international terrorism of concern is the access all groups have to destructive technology. This leads to the threat of unconventional weapons and cyber terrorism, which I discuss throughout the book. These two threats by themselves cause concerns in counterterrorism operations since both could cause mass casualties.

Because of the change in terrorism operations, the Federal Bureau of Investigation has been designated as the lead agency for all terrorism incidents, including prevention of terrorist acts both internationally and domestically. The Department of State is the primary agency for overseas operation, unless it is a military campaign (Schaffer 1940). The FBI strategy for counterterrorism is to prevent acts of terrorism before they occur and to react to the attacks by bringing suspects to justice. In an international situation, the State Department expects the same strategy to be used by the hosting government where an American diplomatic mission is located.

The Federal Bureau of Investigation now combats terrorism in three areas. They are: international terrorism, domestic terrorism, and terrorism prevention internationally and domestically. The FBI conducts all operations from the Counterterrorism Center (United

States Intelligence Community 2009). This operations center was established in 1996 due to the increase of domestic attacks that had links to international terrorist organizations. The operations center comprises the intelligence community that collects, analyzes, and disseminates information to law enforcement agencies so there can be a more effective way to counter threats. The combination of federal and local intelligence agencies increase the flow of sharing information. This provides more people in the law enforcement field with experience and special skills to coordinate or direct efforts to prevent or respond to terrorism incidents. The operations center is a tool that leads to tactical objectives that stop or mitigate terrorist incidents. The tactics used in the FBI come from the FBI Terrorism Program. The program's purpose is to identify and catch terrorists prior to attacks. In aspects of catching individuals, it requires a great deal of intelligence leading to organizations that threaten the United States and American interests. This effort prepares the intelligence and counterintelligence communities for success.

Counterterrorism relies on many resources from multiagency liaison efforts internationally and domestically. This leads to communicating information to the Embassy Legal Attaché Program and the Department of Homeland Security Terrorist Threat Warning System. Cooperation and understanding information leads to developing new federal legislation which protects the United States and American interests. In the United States, legislation developed such as the USA Patriot Act contributed to the establishment of the Joint Terrorism Task Force (JTTF) (Congressional Research Service 2007). The FBI is responsible for the JTTF, which is used as a tool to combat terrorism around the country by using a combination of agencies from the local, state, and federal levels. The JTTF being a tool, and local agencies being the actors/operators that carry out the tactics formulated by the JTTF. This task force has prevented attacks and allowed for resources in the country to be utilized more effectively. This successful program has been part of many critical operations, including the investigation of plots to bomb several locations in domestically.

Another tool, which is the equivalent of the JTTF, is the FBI's program known as Legal Attaché, which assists the State Department in the overseas missions in counterterrorism (Department of Justice 2004). This tool concentrates on global terrorism and cannot be successful without cooperation from allied governments around the world. This places the FBI at the same level as Department of State when maintaining diplomatic relations. Both agencies understand the importance of strong diplomatic relationships, and the tactics to combat terrorism by using law enforcement agencies of host nations. In addition to maintaining good relations, the FBI can have immediate first-on-scene presence with the assistance of the State Department if a terrorist incident occurs. If incidents are prevented because terrorists are apprehended, the Attaché Program will ensure that the captured terrorists are returned to the country where the incident occurred, to stand trial for acts of terrorism or for planning acts of terrorism. One such case involved two counterintelligence employees murdered by a Pakistani, who later fled to Pakistan where the FBI arranged his return to the United States for sentencing (Burns 1997).

Outside of military campaigns, overseas military installations fall under the same strategy of the FBI and State Department, but these agencies are limited on jurisdiction authority. Military personnel at installations overseas are obligated to report all discoveries of terrorism acts and planning to the nearest Attaché within the region the installation is located (DoD Antiterrorism 2007). The FBI is still the lead agency, but requires the Department of State liaison to coordinate resources (Force Protection Handbook 2007). The military doesn't get operationally involved unless there has been a declaration of war, but the military has a strong antiterrorism program that all federal installations and military bases use to mitigate or prevent terrorist attacks (Elsea and Grimmett 2011). The military's antiterrorism program is a tool that military commanders, with the assistance of an antiterrorism committee, use to provide guidance, direction, and coordination to protect United States military assets, including civilian contractors and their families (Force Protection Handbook 2007).

The military uses several antiterrorism strategies during peacetime: maintaining liaison with intelligence agencies; ensuring antiterrorism plans comply with the memorandum of agreement (MOA) with host nations; employing the MOA for local mutual aid support; having applicable State Department Force Protection Instructions on hand; ensuring conformity to the Status of Forces Agreement; identifying and coordinating information sharing with Attachés at embassies; identifying organizations with jurisdiction for law enforcement; and ensuring the safety of military service members during operations other than war or campaigns (DoD Antiterrorism 2007). Some of the major difference in counterterrorism overseas versus domestic is the use of military forces. In the United States under statutory authorizations the military can be used to restore and maintain public order, to meet specified contingencies, to cope with emergencies, and to protect the public. This shows the restrictions the military has, unless ordered by the president of the United States in a declaration of war (Elsea and Grimmett 2011).

There are further differences between domestic and overseas counterterrorism. Counterterrorism presents a challenge for the military in peacetime while overseas. The FBI and Department of State face the same difficulties when relying on foreign governments to assist in investigating or apprehending persons suspected of terrorism. In the United States, the FBI and Department of State can initiate any investigation and use available resources as mentioned in the USA Patriot Act, but overseas, good relationships and communication are required with host nations in order to emphasize the importance of a case. The host nation can easily grant or deny cooperation and cause delays that result in negative analysis and collection. The military, FBI, Department of State, and many other federal agencies are only guests of the host nation. The American presence overseas cannot be overly aggressive with host nations or future efforts toward protecting the United States could fail.

The famous philosopher Voltaire wrote, "Each player must accept the cards that life deals him or her. But once in hand one must decide how to play the cards in order to win the game," (Center for Academic

Integrity, n.a.), this applies to counterterrorism efforts. Terrorism is a worldwide problem that needs adapting to, but relationships between law enforcement agencies and the intelligence communities are key components in preventing terrorism and capturing individuals who participate in or plan terrorist attacks. This process is completed through close cooperation with all persons in the counterterrorism network, leading to speedy dissemination of information and effective analysis of terrorism or criminal activity similar to terrorism.

The FBI has become the primary agency in all terrorism cases due to the intensity of international and domestic attacks, but it requires the assistance of many agencies under a framework that entails information sharing and more. The importance of all agencies and the framework involved with counterterrorism are not only prevention, but also the response as a presence to mitigate incidents. Information sharing should not exclude military sources, since some terrorist events lead to the use of military forces as deemed necessary by the president of the United States. The sources available, from foreign intelligence to the JTTF, ensure the protection of the United States and American interests, which is achieved by investigators specially trained in preventing terrorist attacks.

Chapter 2

DOES STRATEGY REQUIRE A FRAMEWORK?

YES, HERE IS why. Democratic governments do not condone terrorism and combating terrorists requires intelligence and cooperation from all agencies in the military and in law enforcement. The United States prefers diplomacy before deadly force, but terrorist organizations have abused that privilege. Terrorism will never end, and it is difficult to predict attacks, but America can always implement prevention measures and share information. While this information is secret, sharing intelligence among required agencies will place the terrorist groups in compromising positions. Whether or not terrorism will be defeated while maintaining democratic values remains to be seen.

Counterterrorism and Intelligence Framework Overview:

The following is my proposed Counterterrorism and Intelligence Framework that combines counterterrorism measures with border security to provide a strong and efficient system through an emphasis on sharing information and assets from all agencies in civil service positions. The State Department, Department of Transportation, and Federal Emergency Management Agency are civil service agencies that would play vital roles in intelligence and counterterrorism in the proposed Framework. The Department of Homeland Security is responsible for identifying key infrastructures that require attention and designating lead agencies for those areas or sectors (Moteff and Parfomak 2004, 7). The State Department is an agency within the intelligence community (Best 2006, 7), but it is not currently in the critical infrastructure framework of Homeland Security. Neither the Department of Transportation nor the Federal Emergency Management Agency is part of Homeland Security, nor do they even have roles in the intelligence community (King 2011).

The current separation between the intelligence community and critical infrastructure agencies could create problems in the future. The purpose of this proposed Framework is to join both communities and identify the roles and responsibilities of the agencies mentioned above, their specific functions, how they would interact, and tools available to the agencies. This will aid in developing policy toward establishing a robust intelligence system and strategically efficient counterterrorism operations to keep the United States safe, protect its citizens, and mitigate situations. Because there are many hands in the cookie jar that could lead to misinterpretation of intelligence and counterterrorism measures, there are agencies that should not be part of the intelligence community.

Primary Agencies in the Framework:

While only the Federal Emergency Management Agency is a member of the Intelligence Community, all three agencies have much to offer in counterterrorism operations. Each agency would have specific roles and responsibilities within the proposed Framework.

The first agency, the Department of State pursues foreign policy through the diplomatic efforts (Department of State 2011). It has a Counter Terrorism Coordinator Office that aids in improving counterterrorism measures at the American borders and overseas (Ginsborg, Scheinin, and Vermeulen 2011). This allows countries to address threats that pertain to America and allied nations.

The mission of the second agency, the Department of Transportation, is to "Serve the United States by ensuring a fast, safe, efficient, accessible and convenient transportation system that meets our vital national interests and enhances the quality of life of the American people, today and into the future (White House 2011)." This includes all roadways, maritime, and railways.

The third agency, the Federal Emergency Management Agency (FEMA) establishes a process and structure for systematic assistance of federal agencies during major disasters. FEMA also considers special circumstances of terrorist incidents. FEMA provides terrorism preparedness funding to state and local government agencies as required by the Emergency Management Performance Grant Program. The sole role and responsibility of FEMA is reducing loss of life and property and protecting the United States by leading or supporting the nation in a comprehensive response and recovery plan. This proposed plan is expected to be risk-based toward emergency, mitigation, and preparedness, and because terrorism is unique, the plan also includes consequence management (FEMA 2007).

Secondary Agencies in the Framework:

There are seventeen agencies that make up the Intelligence Community (Gottlied 2011). Two of the agencies have a small responsibility toward counterterrorism compared to DOS, DOT, and FEMA. They are the National Geospatial Intelligence Agency and the National Reconnaissance Office. In the proposed Framework, these two agencies would be removed from intelligence and counterterrorism operations. The National Geospatial Intelligence Agency is a high-technology imagery intelligence service (National Geospatial-Intelligence Agency 2011). This technology-derived data is analyzed and results in intelligence that locates, identifies, or describes distinctive targeted interests. The Central Intelligence Agency (CIA), the Department of Defense (DoD), and the Defense Intelligence Agency (DIA) have the same capability. The National Reconnaissance Office, according to their website, "is the US government agency in charge of designing, building, launching, and maintaining America's intelligence satellites." (National Reconnaissance Office 2011, website). This is a good asset for the United States, but not an agency that requires connection to the Intelligence Community, especially when they assist foreign governments in the same technologies.

The Functions of Primary Agencies in the Framework:

If DOS, DOT, and FEMA are approved for the Counterterrorism and Intelligence Community, combined with the critical infrastructure framework, they will have the following specific functions that will aid the mission of Counterterrorism and Intelligence:

1. The Department of State will ensure protection of passenger liners against hijacking, establish maritime security standards of United States and Foreign combined ports, and ensure travel advisories are issued to Americans against unsafe ports (Department of State 2011A). Under the Intelligence Reform Act, DOS is responsible for cruise liners by verifying that passenger checks are conducted against a comprehensive coordinated database containing information of known terrorists and associates (Public Law 108-458, 2004). The same efforts provided to maritime, jetliners, and cruise liners should also be applied to the United States borders and screening points of international airports.

2. The Department of Transportation is currently overlaps with Homeland Security (Find Law 2002). Homeland Security is the lead agency for response to transportation situations involving terrorism or suspected terrorism (National Response Framework 2008). The lead agency should be the Department of Transportation. If the DOT is placed into the intelligence community, it will provide terrorism prevention measures for United States harbor channels inland, intra-coastal and coastal waterways, passenger and cargo terminals, underground pipelines, all railways, and domestic and international freight (The White House 2011). This would most likely place the DOT as the largest enforcement agency of transportation laws and counterterrorism.

3. Federal Emergency Management Agency (FEMA) is the specialist in emergency response. If FEMA becomes part of the Intelligence Community, it will provide training to the Department of Defense, military, and civil service employees of federal, state, and local agencies in Emergency Response to Terrorism and Mitigation (FEMA 592, 2007). FEMA will also ensure its responsibility to all states by providing response assistance in ten regions for weapons of mass destruction by using teams called Civil Support (FEMA 592, 2007). The team will establish exercises for federal, state, and local governments. They will also educate federal and local governments in the handling of domestic terrorism and how to respond to consequences of unconventional attacks. FEMA would assist local jurisdictions in law enforcement and secure critical infrastructures. The primary purpose of FEMA is research and development in all aspects of predictive response, mitigation, and recovery of disaster (Goss 1996). The DOS, the DOT, and FEMA have special functions that aid the Intelligence Community and need to be driving forces in the Critical Infrastructure Sector of Department of Homeland Security.

Resources and Tools:

The three agencies have overlapping responsibilities that provide thorough interaction and support of resources. The interaction of agencies will require information sharing and resource management. What makes this area difficult is the budget, and many emergency service sectors have experienced this problem. Regardless, technology has made it easy for services to communicate national infrastructure concerns. DOS, DOT, FEMA use the National Infrastructure Coordinating Center through the World Wide Web. The access to the online media serves as the central point of notifications regarding infrastructure threats, disruptions, intrusions, and suspicious activity. The agency or emergency sector personnel are required in this online media to report any incident or attacks involving their infrastructures.

In the proposed Framework, the DOS, the DOT, and FEMA will share resources, since budgets are shrinking and problems are growing.

According to PBS's *Frontline* there are important intelligence and counterterrorism tools available to the agencies proposed in this framework. The first one is the Foreign Intelligence Surveillance Act (Carpenter, Felch, Moughty, Sandler, and Temchine 2003). This act allows the government to obtain a warrant to serve against any reasonable suspicion of intelligence threat so surveillance can legally be conducted to receive information that threatens national security.

The second tool is the USA Patriot Act (Carpenter, Felch, Moughty, Sandler, and Temchine 2003). This act allows law enforcement the leeway of searches and information collection of electronics when an investigation is showing trends or suspicion of terrorism.

The third tool is the Attorney General Guidelines (Carpenter, Felch, Moughty, Sandler, and Temchine 2003). This gives directors of federal agencies the privilege to notify the attorney general of any intelligence concerns that require immediate attention.

The fourth tool is the FISA Court Opinion (Carpenter, Felch, Moughty, Sandler, and Temchine 2003). Opinions of the court aid agencies on approaches to criminal activity versus terrorist activity and not mixing the two during investigations. The courts did not want agencies to abuse a flexible law that is already being questioned as unconstitutional.

The fifth tool available is the Material Support Statute (Carpenter, Felch, Moughty, Sandler, and Temchine 2003). The statute allows prosecutors to increase prison sentences of individuals who conduct smuggling of any material to any terrorist organization.

The sixth tool available is the Enemy Combatant Designation (Carpenter, Felch, Moughty, Sandler, and Temchine 2003). This allows for terrorists to receive trials under the justice system as combatants per the third Geneva Convention.

There is one tool available that the United States Marine Corps provides to all federal agencies in the event that a chemical or biological incident occurs. The marines can obtain support and logistics from the Chemical/Biological Incident Response Force (CBIRF). CBIRF is an element of United States Marine Corps in Indian Head, Maryland. It deploys on short notice in the United States and overseas to respond to credible threats of chemical, biological, radiation, and nuclear events.

Policy Recommendations:

The Department of Homeland Security has many areas to oversee and participate in operationally while securing the United States. There are four policies this proposed Framework recommends that the Department of Homeland Security should adopt. The first is that the Department of Homeland Security should add the Department of State, the Department of Transportation, and the Federal Emergency Management Agency to the key infrastructure Framework to build resources for supplying intelligence and counterterrorism efforts. This will make the Intelligence and Counterterrorism Framework stronger to combat future attacks.

The second recommendation would be for The Department of State to maintain diplomacy by gaining information pertaining to other countries' threats and using the sourced information to prevent most threats from arriving in the United States via the international airports. This leads to the tracking of visitors, and intercepting passport and visa fraud. The United States cannot track alone, so it is imperative to have international support.

The third policy recommendation concerns the nation's railways. The Department of Transportation can establish a Highway Enforcement Department for all States that the Department of Homeland Security can oversee in efforts to provide more law-enforcement coverage to enforce traffic laws on state and federal highways and all railways. The Highway Enforcement Department would also be a responding unit to emergencies of critical infrastructures or assets to state and local governments and would conduct terrorism assessments on the scene.

This same effort would tie into the Federal Emergency Management Agency, since emergency services require roadways to respond to emergency incidents.

The last policy recommendation to the Department of Homeland Security is to provide special training and support to first responders to protect communities from the effects of terrorism. First responders lack assistance and information about threats in their jurisdictions. Terrorists' destructive ability has been seen through the use of explosives. Emergency service first responders must be prepared to handle secondary devices or other threats while maintaining the initial responder's ability to control the scene and save lives.

Similar to the recommended procedures for the Department of Highway Enforcement, local fire, police, and ambulance services should implement designation of Terrorism Liaison Officers to concentrate on the perimeter and beyond of emergency scenes for unusual activity characterized as possible terrorism surveillance. This recommendation for policy allows for more citizens to be hired to protect those who serve communities in emergency civil service occupations as specialists in terrorism reporting and recording. Their responsibilities would be:

1. Conduct skill training necessary for public safety and security personnel tasked with terrorism prevention and response.

2. Provide information of contemporary terrorism and a basic understanding of methods used by terrorists in targeting facilities and facility occupants.

3. Examination of the unique methods used by terrorists in executing explosive attacks.

4. Provide security and law enforcement professionals with a thorough understanding of terrorist methodology and the risks associated with explosive devices.

5. Identify threat of chemical and biological terrorism and provide a thorough review of the types of agents that terrorists may employ in attacks and the spectrum of methods used by terrorists in attacking facilities with chemical and biological (CB) agents.

6. Conduct surveys of countermeasures and identify countermeasures used in anti-terrorism planning to control risk by reducing risk probability and risk criticality.

7. Identify the unique methods used by terrorists to gather target intelligence and effective countermeasures for impeding and detecting intelligence collection.

8. Provide assistant anti-terrorism officers with an understanding of the measures used to protect facilities against overt, covert, and deceptive entry attacks.

9. Identify guidelines and model procedures for conducting comprehensive screening and searching of facility for those who go inside, and a wide range of techniques used by terrorists in circumventing detection at access control stations and practices used by many organizations at risk of terrorist attack.

10. Train working groups regarding the terrorist and criminal use of mail bombs and contaminated mailings and effective strategies for intercepting and responding to hazardous mail incidents.

11. Provide anti-terrorism working groups with a safe and realistic guidelines for responding to terrorist events and aiding emergency responders with the early stages of critical incident management.

Framework Conclusion:

The Department of Homeland Security remains a work in progress, and infrastructure and national security information sharing will continue to build new relationships within the emergency service arena. The intelligence and counterterrorism community requires communication and human contact regardless of the unique issues of security and privacy.

Counterterrorism must be layered with defenses. The defenses are deterrence, intelligence, prevention, and mitigation. DOS, DOT, and FEMA are agencies that can act preemptively in all areas. This is why they need to be part of the Intelligence Community and Homeland Security Critical Infrastructure. The DOS, the DOT, and FEMA can accomplish protective, preparatory measures, planning, and protecting of critical infrastructures. The United States knows that terrorism is real and predicting the next attack is difficult, but prevention and information sharing can be attempted to mitigate disastrous results. The combination of the Department of State, the Department of Transportation, and the Federal Emergency Management Agency will benefit Homeland Security Intelligence and Counterterrorism. Another agency that many people are not aware of is the Department of Energy. This agency has more to lose than gain as it provides energy to the American people.

Chapter 3

WHAT ROLE DOES THE DEPARTMENT OF ENERGY PLAY?

HERE IS AN under looked importance: For more than fifty years, the Department of Energy (DOE) has provided intense security for all assets domestically and internationally in order to protect American interests (DOE, NEST). The September 11, 2001 terror attacks on the New York World Trade Center Buildings and the Pentagon brought new momentum to security in all DOE facilities that store nuclear weapons. This new momentum ramped up the functional roles of counterterrorism by DOE and many federal agencies in the intelligence community (DOE). As the functional roles changed, so did all assets and tools available for all agencies to conduct counterterrorism operations.

Changing assets and tools available to counterterrorism activities brought new interactions between separate agencies that never previously had an intelligence role and to a collective group that now shares information and resources. This has placed the Department of Justice in a position to identify implications of available counterterrorism tools so federal agencies can achieve proactive investigations that lead to discovery of suspicious activity perceived as terrorism related (DOJ). All agencies' involvement in counterterrorism and support from the Department of Justice allows for immediate emergency response to emergencies initiated by terrorist action, which will ultimately minimize casualties within the jurisdiction in which a situation occurs.

Department of Energy Functions:

A counterterrorism function provided by the Department of Energy is the assessment of worldwide nuclear terrorism threats and nuclear proliferation and constant evaluation of foreign technology threats (DOE). This applies to domestic protection because counterintelligence operations protect all nuclear weapons, facilities, and scientific research, including those on American soil.

Another serious function the DOE has is performing analysis of energy security-related intelligence issues that support United States national security, policies, programs, and objectives. The DOE plays a major role in the intelligence community by contributing to counterterrorism. The DOE also plays a major role in the domestic critical infrastructure by using DOE laboratories to help utilities and industrial associations create security assessments. These assessments contribute to the security of water utilities, chemical storage plants, dams, and power supply facilities.

Tools the Department of Energy Uses:

Tools available to the agency to conduct counterterrorism operations stem from the DOE's Department of Emergency Response. This department manages radiological emergency support if there is need for crisis management or incidents involving weapons of mass destruction. This department is ready at a moment's notice to respond to such incidents. It is important that DOE has this type of responsibility so it can communicate threat assessment and nuclear safety concerns and coordinate any assistance in nonproliferation. The tools the department has are Aerial Measuring System, Atmospheric Release Advisory Capability, Accident Response Group, Federal Radiological Monitoring Assessment Center, Nuclear Emergency Search Teams,

Radiological Assistance Program, Radiation Emergency Assistance Center and Training Site, and Nuclear Incident Response (DOE, NEST).

Arial Measuring Systems operate from within an aircraft or a helicopter that tracks, monitors, and takes samples of radioactive plumes or measures material deposits on the ground that can be radioactive (DOE, AMS). Atmospheric Release Advisory Capability is a computer system that is operated by the Lawrence Livermore National Laboratory, and the system identifies what is released into the atmosphere or environment (Sullivan 1993). Accident Response Groups are the primary responders to all domestic nuclear incidents involving nuclear weapons, so they can control and recover or even advise on-scene commanders of actions required (DOE, ARG). The Assessment Center's principle function is to identify major radiological emergencies that affect America so any lead federal agency can receive proper support for affected areas (Hurley and Thome 1996). The Nuclear Emergency Search Team responds to all terrorism situations involving nuclear energy and radiological material so they can support operations of suspected nuclear explosive devices (Nettles 1991). The Radiological Assistance Program is ran by a group of equipped and trained individuals who respond to and provide resources that mitigate perceived radiation hazards (DOE, RAP). The Radiation Emergency Assistance Center and Training Site provides twenty-four-hour response service, which supports medical treatment for radiological emergencies (DOE, REAC/TS). Communicated Threat Credibility Assessment provides technical support operationally on behavioral assessments of threat directed against the United States and United States interests.

The Department of Energy in Cooperation with other Government Agencies:

In the past the Department of Energy did not interact well with other agencies, even though they all conduct similar intelligence collection and counterterrorism strategies. The Department of Energy established a program called Nuclear Counterterrorism, which works with other federal agencies to eliminate terrorists' ability in making improvised nuclear bombs (DOE). Three of the agencies the DOE work with are the Federal Bureau of Investigation, the Department of Defense, and the Federal Emergency Management Agency. The DOE has only a supporting role when interacting with other agencies to perform counterterrorism operations, and will "provide scientific-technical personnel and equipment in support of the lead federal agency during all aspects of a nuclear/radiological Weapons of Mass Destruction terrorist incident" (CONPLAN, Page 4). DoD and DOE share the responsibility of research and counterterrorism (Friedman, page 1). This responsibility leads to information sharing and collecting. They also assist each other in threat assessments leading to terrorism prevention.

One federal agency that the DOE works well with primarily in international affairs is the Department of State. The DOE produces and disseminates foreign intelligence and participates in intelligence collection and analysis (Executive Order 12333). This is a must for the DOE and all agencies that participate in the intelligence community. While the interaction the DOE has with Department of State may largely be regarding foreign matters, the Executive Order 12333 is also used for domestic affairs.

The Executive Order and USA Patriot Act direct that the intelligence community needs to obtain reliable information to protect America, including DOE's nuclear facilities, using all means available and with due regard for all citizens of the United States (The National Strategy for Homeland Security 2002). DOE and all agencies that they interact with must give special emphasis to detecting and countering espionage and other threats or activities that jeopardize the United States using terrorism (CONPLAN, Page 3).

The Justice Department support of available counterterrorism tools has benefited not only the DOE but also all federal agencies with intelligence gathering and sharing abilities through the USA Patriot Act (The National Strategy for Homeland Security 2002), but any alleged terrorist activity under 22 USC 7211, Public Law

107-56, will be prosecuted by the Department of Justice (DOJ 2008). President George W. Bush, with Congressional action, made all efforts to combine counterterrorism tools from all agencies with law enforcement authority. DOE is one of many agencies with law enforcement authority. The only scrutiny the Department of Justice is receiving from the public is the use of law enforcement against terrorists, but any tools at the disposal of the United States to prevent terrorism are a true legitimate way to detain or investigate terrorism activities. (Kris).

The Department of Energy can easily coordinate with emergency responders to minimize casualties by having a good working relationship with the Center for Disease Control (CDC). The CDC is the lead federal agency that responds to a radiological incident. The DOE and the CDC together can assess and monitor people's health in the midst of an incident. Both agencies must ensure the safety of all responders in order to save lives within the community. First responders need assistance from CDC and DOE to take precautionary measures to keep each other alive. The DOE also has working knowledge of effects radiological incidents can have on food, so they will ensure all food is safe to consume during such a disaster. Moreover, both agencies will be advisors to emergency responders to provide sound information on medical and public health so people's health is protected.

The intelligence community is growing fast due to the current international and domestic threat, (NNSAA 2004). The attacks of September 11, 2001 brought many changes to the intelligence field and new directorates in the homeland security field. These directorates are bureaucracies that can add more stress to the collection process in protecting America. In theory, simple is easier, but the American intelligence community has increased the strain and collection process so more eyes and ears are analyzing conditions for decision makers (NNSAA 2004). The DOE is doing well as a partner in the intelligence community and even better in the antiterrorism force protection arena. Force protection is one of many functions the DOE has responsibility for, since they must protect nuclear research and development in the United States. Nuclear energy will continue to be a target of interest to the enemies of the United States, and this is why it is important that DOE is a member of the intelligence community. Their membership in the past was rough as they interacted with other federal agencies, but they hold solid relationships with FEMA, FBI, and DOD as they support the spirit of the Patriot Act and Executive Order 12333. This synergy of agencies will preserve and protect American citizens from grave danger without violating civil liberties and will also support emergency first responders in the minimizing of life loss during nuclear, biological, and radiological disasters.

Chapter 4

ARE CIVIL LIBERTIES BEING VIOLATED?

THE WORLD CONTINUES to be threatening by terrorist activity, and this activity has taken its toll on America. With safety in question, it will be difficult to balance the constitutional rights of Americans and provide thorough security procedures that deter or prevent terrorist activity. America's current security perspective has changed, and protecting America is a must through the United States Patriot Act, U.S. PATRIOT Act means Uniting and Strengthening America by Providing Appropriate Tools Required to Intercept and Obstruct Terrorism. Opponents of the Patriot Act have criticized it as being unjust to the American people. This opposition can cause more concern as America becomes more prone to attacks. The Patriot Act supports law-enforcement officials to be more aggressive in tracking crime that leads to terrorist related activity and even to stop terrorist attacks. The Patriot Act allows law-enforcement officials to gather, analyze, and disseminate information as it pertains to investigating operations of, and response to, terrorist activity or attacks. Noticeably, terrorists have infected American society with fear, and their success will ultimately continue to fuel their efforts. It is important for Americans to understand how the Patriot Act can deter or prevent terrorist activity and attacks.

Historically, the common weapons of choice for terrorists were chemical and biological. Chemical and biological agents could be delivered through well water, use of herbs, and dead remains of animals or human beings. Today, terrorists are primarily using explosives. I have concern that biological and chemical agents will be joined with explosive capability.

The terrorist attacks of September 11, 2001 introduced a new means of explosive capability through an airliner full of fuel. This proved that terrorists have nothing but time to plan an effective attack on any demographic. As devastating a blow those attacks were, it is fortunate that the plans did not also include any biological or chemical weapons. Terrorists can effectively complete a purchase to support a mission by blending into society. They only use cash, and they act and dress according to the culture they are working in. Terrorists are knowledgeable and are able to strike under any premises to prevent being caught by law enforcement. This kind of activity is better known as cell operations. These cell operations are the reason for increased security in the United Stated of America. Increased security has placed law-enforcement agencies in a position to develop and change procedures to prevent or even react to terrorist activity so civil rights are not violated (Roper 2003).

The need for law enforcement to change procedures to prevent civil liability is not the only challenge the United States is facing as it fights terrorism. Another significant challenge is the emotional stress the American people continue to experience. Through the media, America witnessed the attacks on the World Trade Centers during September 11, 2001. The attacks introduced a level of emotional stress that can be translated to Post-Traumatic Stress Disorder (PTSD), especially for those living in New York City at the time. A study reported in the August 7, 2002 issue of *The Journal of American Medical Association* stated that 11 percent of New York City residents had PTSD from the attacks that took place on September 11, 2001 (Schlenger, Caddell, Ebert, and Jordan 2002). The residents suffering from the attacks ranged from children to elderly folk, but the children were more affected by the attacks (Schlenger, Caddell, Ebert, and

Jordan 2002). Chapter 15 will elaborate more on the emotional toll our country has suffered due to terrorism and natural disasters.

September 11, 2001 may have introduced evil acts from terrorist operatives, but on October 26, 2001 Congress passed the United and Strengthening America by Providing Appropriate Tools Required to Interrupt and Obstruct Terrorism Act of 2001 (USA PATRIOT Act) (Roper 2003). The USA Patriot Act intended to provide change to national security. This also led to changes to criminal and immigration laws (Roper 2003). The purpose behind the USA Patriot Act was to allow law enforcement the means required to deter and prevent terrorism in America, and at the same time, protect Americans' civil liberties since the Act allowed law enforcement officials to conduct surveillance or collect information as it pertains to trends of terrorists from any person involved with computer crimes and violent crimes (Henderson 2002).

The USA Patriot Act is one of many specific measures used by the Bush Administration to prevent or deter terrorism activity in America. On October 29, 2001, there was an inclusion to the Act to assist law enforcement in tracking terrorism activity through financing. This inclusion was called the Homeland Security Presidential Directive -2 (HSPD-2). Another measure established on November 27, 2002 was the National Commission on Terrorist Attacks through the United States (Public Law 107-306). This public law allowed law enforcement to investigate "facts and circumstances relating to the terrorist attacks of September 11, 2001" (Kamien 2006).

The 9/11 Commission on July 22, 2004 published a report to President Bush with recommendations on preparedness measures designed to guard America from future attacks. On December 8, 2004, President Bush signed those recommendations into law. It was called the Intelligence Reform and Terrorism Prevention Act of 2004 (IRTPA), which allowed for reforms to become effective called the Foreign Intelligence Surveillance Act (FISA) so any terrorist that purchases or collect materials illegally will be prosecuted. The IRTPA also opened opportunity in the intelligence community to prevent proliferation of weapons of mass destruction. The joint Intelligence Community Council assisted the Defense National Intelligence (DNI) in creating the Privacy and Civil Liberties Oversight Board with in the Executive Office (Kamien 2006). This shows the effort President Bush took to prevent or deter terrorism, and approves counter measures into law.

Protecting America soon had additional problems, as President Bush was quick to develop policies to prevent terrorist attacks (Kamien 2006). This was evident by the opinions Americans had regarding their civil liberties; 7 states and 399 towns and villages adapted resolutions condemning various Patriot Act provisions (Herman 2002). According to Herman's 2002 article, "USA Patriot Act and Submajoritarian Fourth Amendment," one area that the American people are concerned about is their Fourth Amendment (searches and seizures) rights. The Fourth Amendment to the Constitution states that:

> The right of the people to be secure on their person, houses, papers, and effects, against unreasonable search and seizure shall not be violated, and no warrant shall be issued, but upon probable cause, supported by oath or affirmation, and particularly describing the place to be searched and the persons or things to be seized. (as cited in Ranalli 2009, 15)

This clarifies that law enforcement officials will specifically check for items as it relates to terrorist activity or trends and even regular crimes. If property is seized, it will only be used as purpose of evidence in criminal prosecution (Herman 2002). Moreover, it is the surveillance portion of the USA Patriot Act that intimidates Americans.

The Fourth Amendment mentions reasonable expectation of privacy (Henderson 2002). Regardless if an American citizen is a terrorist or day-to-day citizen, all persons have rights (Henderson 2002). The USA Patriot Acts provides law enforcement officials may use surveillance as a tool to deter or prevent terrorism; this has been proven to falter in Katz vs. United States (389 U. S. 347) when federal law-enforcement agents placed electronic devices in telephone booths (Ranalli 2009). This action by law-enforcement officials went against reasonable expectation and privacy as per the United States Constitution. The American people need to trust that law enforcement is not conducting surveillance on all people but using resources to identify terrorist trends and activity.

Events throughout the world will always cause laws to change. As Miller stated, "the United States government was confronted with a serious problem that surrounded the searching of passengers of airliners" (2004). Homeland Security was searching people for explosives because of a Chechen woman, who in 2004 carried explosives onto two different airliners where they later detonated (Miller 2004). This proved that security procedures after September 11, 2001 still needed improvement since detectors could not identify plastic explosives. Homeland Security purchased screeners that scan the contours of the body, and Americans believed that this was a privacy violation of their rights but others argued that all procedures taken are necessary to protect Americans (Miller 2004). President Bush and his Administration were not attempting to violate Americans' rights but instead had probable cause to protect America from terrorist attacks.

The USA Patriot Act allows airport law-enforcement officials to conduct counterterrorism measures by being proactive in protecting America (Kamien 2006). Another item that the USA Patriot Act provides is authorizing law-enforcement officials to be the hub in monitoring electronic sources like e-mail and voice messages and in gathering personal information from medical physicians, libraries, and banks (Kamien 2006). This is only done if a person shows terrorist trends or true terrorist activity, and law enforcement officials can do this with no proof provided to courts until all information proves to be case worthy. An added benefit to this authority is the ability for law-enforcement officials to freeze the accounts of any person they are investigating with no explanation, so a case can be built to prove wrongdoing as it relates to terrorism (Kamien 2006).

Terrorism is hard to identify when there are many interpretations of what terrorism is. Terrorism is not classified as a crime unless there is unlawful use of force and violence against people or damage to property that places governments in difficult political positions (National Security Division 1998). The USA Patriot Act that the Bush Administration established to protect America can be considered a terrorism prevention tool (Kamien 2006). Terrorism prevention will always have challenges as terrorists plan attacks by understanding laws and specifically targeting groups in society for a greater impact. While attacks take place and the kinds of attacks change, so will laws in an effort to keep America safe. The USA Patriot Act may raise many questions in the minds of Americans as a result of the inconvenience that counterterrorism measures cause, but the mission is ultimately to prevent terrorist acts.

Evaluating the Fourth Amendment as it relates to the Patriot Act, there is no proof that Americans are to have their constitutional rights violated. Americans should not become prejudiced against measures that defend from terrorist activity or attacks. Terrorists are operating covertly within America's borders to compromise the United States (Henderson 2002), but all those who are American citizens, terrorist or not, will be interviewed in accordance to the Constitution of the United States. It is nothing but deterrence that the Bush Administration developed by establishing departments and laws to oversee and prevent terrorist activity. This includes the processing and receiving of information pertaining to open cases related to suspected terrorism. The initiative that the Bush Administration took to protect the United States does not violate the Constitution. Instead it places law enforcement in a position to provide a sense of homeland security, while all civil rights conditions are screened and reviewed to protect American interests (Roper 2003).

All law-enforcement agencies nationwide have a difficult task in preventing terrorism or crimes leading to suspected terrorism, as terrorism will continue and may seem to have no end. As long as all law-enforcement agencies involved in counterterrorism share information and work together (National Security Division 1998),

America will have a better chance of staying safe. When another attack is attempted or does take place, all agencies will have full integration of the intelligence through investigation as they operate and respond to such a crisis. In 2010, there were eleven attempts against Americans on American soil prevented under the authority of the USA Patriot Act due to the flexibility provided to law enforcement (Herman 2002).

The United States will continue to face challenges when preventing terrorism while preserving the Constitution. The tactics of terrorists are becoming more efficient, as Americans fear worse attacks than September 11, 2001. Americans who lived near the incidents continue to suffer from PTSD as documented by doctors. This is truly the psychological effect terrorists enjoy. Incidents like September 11 and the bombing of Russian planes only prompt more intrusive laws to protect innocent people.

After researching the Patriot Act and the actions law enforcement is taking to protect America, there is no question that the Fourth Amendment and reasonable expectation of privacy are being protected appropriately and individuals are not persecuted against their will, unless they are suspected of crimes leading to terrorism activity. Knowing this to be true, the American people should be proud to have the Foreign Intelligence Surveillance Act, which deters opportunity to make or acquire products that could be used to construct weapons of mass destruction. The USA Patriot Act not only prevents WMD from being acquired, but it also provides law enforcement the means of establishing preparedness measures toward terrorism by collecting, analyzing, and disseminating information as it pertains to investigating, operations of, and response to terrorist activity or attacks. Terrorist groups receive most of their direct support from established auxiliary cells developed in countries around the world. Terrorism is not going away, and one of our own citizens could be related to a terrorism cell and would likely argue freedom of speech against the Patriot Act and privacy laws to find legal protection for their actions.

As terrorism continues to rage against the innocence of the American citizens, many rights that the American Constitution and Bill of Rights set in stone are possibly being jeopardized. One of these areas in a compromising situation is the First Amendment. Our First Amendment provides the opportunity to communicate without government censor controls. Communication is used to ease concerns the American people may have about current events or political issues globally and nationally (Viotti). The media is the mastermind of such communication. Even though the media alerts listeners to immediate crisis, it can also place fear. It is necessary to keep Americans informed at the same time as to educate the importance of homeland security and ensuring that accurate accounts of a crisis are being relayed to the American people as it happens.

Under the First Amendment, freedom of press has become a vital tool in providing information to Americans (Kamien 2006). There is no longer the official news reporter on the ground reporting current information that is deemed important by the press corporation. Today's technology makes the Internet the primary worldwide communication network. Eyewitness reporters are selling their information to news agencies and allow the topic to be officially broadcasted. This has benefited America when dealing with freedom of the press and freedom of speech (Kamien 2006). In addition to eyewitness reporting, Internet blogging has become popular nationwide and globally (Viotti). This is another benefit of freedom of expression and freedom of speech. Information about how to handle an emergency situation or crisis has been posted to the Internet for the majority of Americans to read. Media sites even provide links to the ready.gov website that assist in making emergency kits when current news broadcasts announce disaster (Kamien 2006). Today's technology through the Internet, video reporting, and even texting on cell phones has made it easier for the media and Americans to alert each other during disaster and crisis faster than the traditional reporter waiting for air time (Kamien 2006). This simply leads to saving more lives, conveying vital information, and contributing to an orderly emergency response.

Technology being used by the media and Americans may provide current information, yet it also provides dramatic consequences. One such consequence is inaccurate information, which is a distraction to citizens as they attempt to understand a crisis. This distraction can easily lead to destructive results because people fear the unknown (Bullock and Coppola 2009). The unknown and the use of the Internet offer dramatic expression to a current crisis when Americans are unsure what the media is providing. This intensifies immediacy and emotion (Bullock and Coppola 2009). Another concern evolves politicians and public emotions as the media captures the feeling and makes a headline in relation to the current crisis or disaster. The general public will believe what they see and hear on TV, radio, and the Internet. Technology has benefits for media use, but it fails the media competition by making reporting faster and stronger. Reporters may struggle to get information broadcasted as soon as possible but fail in the accuracy of events that have unfolded. This action places Americans in a position of misunderstanding of a crisis that may require people to react to (Bullock and Coppola 2009).

Inaccurate information and too much information provided by the media and eyewitness reporters, e.g. unofficial reporters or sources, is protected by the First Amendment, but may have negative effects on citizens who require news of crisis and disaster with no dramatic race to the first broadcast or receiving of information as it is occurring (Bullock and Coppola 2009). As much as Americans need information provided accurately, it would be unconstitutional to control the free flow of information through freedom of speech and freedom of the press. The general public must be able to build perspective and context of national and global concern (Bullock and Coppola 2009). Providing information through the media and open sources will allow the public to show the right and wrong in events as they unfold or come to an end (Bullock and Coppola 2009). If free speech is curtailed during times of crisis or even war, the American people will not feel a part of the solution that the United States is involved in.

Terrorism and crisis will continue, and we will not be able to stop them. The First Amendment provides much latitude in the way

Americans can express information, but it is obvious of dramatic reporting of disaster that is displayed by eager individuals presenting inexperienced thought to America. As long as education continues to be available, it is truly on each American to understand their rights. If they choose to not research appropriately, the remaining population shouldn't suffer from another's mistake in voicing improper judgment to the public. The media has much benefit to communicate to the population of listeners on an immediate crisis in a calm professional manner without causing panic.

Here is a statement from me regarding the topic: Most Americans are consumed by their work and daily life, and the luxury the media has to influence viewers goes beyond the time available of many people to conduct open research on topics of interests regarding governmental issues. The more people know leads to less complaining about political issues but allows for intelligent resolve if accepted.

With this in mind, there are many Fox or CNN shows regarding money and more. Why can't there be segments that discuss homeland security for viewers. This could scale up to international interests, but the opportunity to educate viewers on current policies and what policies mean and to offer interviews with experts in the field benefit would all law enforcement agencies, emergency services, and politicians. Americans should be aware of the hardship behind assuring homeland security. Most Americans are aware of www.white house.com and other informational websites, but it is hard to look for something on the web if you don't generally understand what to search for. The web is tricky that way—it is also compromising and addicting, but people fail to find accurate information since the web-attention span is lost within the Google searches.

If it were possible for me to educate America on homeland security issues and policies that aid homeland security, other than this book, I would call my segment "The Fight Within." My segment would last no longer than thirty minutes. The segment would focus on homeland security issues, recent laws passed, H.R. reviews, and what they mean. Many Americans are also unaware of court proceedings involving terrorism cases. It would be important to present recent trials at state and federal levels, and answer questions that Americans are blogging. Terrorists take advantage of the media, why can't Americans who earned that right under the First Amendment also use the media to their advantage?

I won't be surprised if police officers start handcuffing people for officer safety reasons due to what terrorism has done to the constitutional rights.

If a person from any nation and culture chooses to move to the United States, they are choosing the American lifestyle. If I moved to another nation from the United States, would I be accepted as America accepts others?

Chapter 5

DOES TERRORISM RELY ON THE MEDIA?

ABSOLUTELY . . . I DISCUSSED the First Amendment in Chapter 4. This chapter doesn't go against press reporters, but amplifies the importance of their duties. The twenty-first century has a dramatic increase of terrorism ranging from suicide bombings, missile strikes, and random shootings. Terrorism attacks place the lives of the public, emergency responders, police, and military at risk, but innocent civilians suffer the most loss. Around the world all people react in horror when attacks are made against civilians. Attacking civilians is morally wrong, and the broadcasting of attacks by the media can trigger memories and cause mental-health conditions to progress. This leads to the fear people have regarding terrorism due to the media reports from terrorist incidents.

The media plays an important role for the public. The outlet capability provided by television, newspaper, radio, and the Internet have a well-developed means of network communications that can't be mirrored. The public expects the media to provide accurate and timely information, which is supported by the First Amendment of the United States Constitution, but many people who live in America do not have a basic understanding of the First Amendment. Even if our government supports the media, media does affect all people, children in particular, negatively when disaster hits.

The media in today's world plays a profound role as it carries the burden of the frontlines of information as it happens. This is a unique responsibility the media has, since the public requires news during crisis. The society trusts the media to provide information. This information is the pipeline from which the community learns of events, and especially when terrorism is likely, the public will be glued to the media. The power of the media to assist in social order and the psychological impact it has on individuals like emergency responders and the general public is beyond the scope of the immediate victim. If the media delivers bad information, it can be distracting and destructive. For example: the events that took place after September 11, 2001 involved inaccurate stories provided by the media. This distracted first responders and brought unnecessary emotional pain to victims and families on edge due to the attacks on the World Trade Centers (Aleshinloye 2011).

Another psychological effect that impacts individuals is the technology of today; it increases immediacy and emotional responses to include fear or anger. Images provided by the media can be disturbing. Allowing the general public to become possible reporters using wireless communication like cell phones and Blackberries (eyewitness reporting) poses a problem, because authorities are not offered the opportunity to screen a broadcast for accuracy before it is reported. That can cause more fear in the community than necessary, spread rumors, and start errors of information. Terrorism magnifies emotions and information, which causes the public to want more news about terrorist attacks. Eyewitness reporting can sometimes be beneficial to the general public, yet it can psychologically impact people involved in disasters or terrorism attacks.

Victims of attacks, recovery teams, and first responders to attacks have different exposure to events, which impacts them psychologically in different ways. Victims of terrorism attacks suffer similar effects as first responders, because they are participants in recovery efforts provided by emergency first responders.

Victims are present for attacks. The psychological effects off attacks will most likely lead to Post Traumatic Stress Disorder (Mathewson 2011). Among other symptoms, this condition causes jumpiness and sleepless nights. Sleepless nights also affect recovery teams. Recovery teams with no sleep continuously work scenes to find body parts. Recovery team members will suffer similar effects as first responders from psychological distress (Mathewson 2011). First responders become more involved than most people because they push themselves to their limits physically and emotionally.

The Red Cross has identified that 52 percent of emergency first responders are suffering from mental health conditions (Mathewson 2011). Regardless of their roles during events, members from each type of survivors of terrorist attacks occupy themselves with outside activities to solitude after their trauma (Mathewson 2011). The majority of survivors treat themselves to massages and other activities to prevent or limit exposure to media coverage (Mathewson 2011). The purpose of limiting media exposure is to prevent mourning of losses, which trigger the memories.

Terrorism is magnified more than necessary by the media, which causes fears and feelings of the unexpected from people. Broadcasting terrorist activities should be limited to reduce such impacts. This is mentioned since most people will experience mediated terrorism through television, and radio; other sources that people absorb news and information are through the Internet, such as pictures and even online articles from journalist. When this type of information is available during disaster or terrorist attacks, it affects people but shouldn't affect the freedom of information and freedom of speech that the United States provides.

In reality, most attacks truly do not receive media coverage (Kern, Just, and Norris 2003, 40). The combination of terrorism and media provides opportunities, but also involves risks. The opportunities outweigh the risk due to the ability to disseminate information to people. This allows people to review multiple sources and gather information to establish viewpoints of the situation, but the public and emergency responders would also feel that they are hostages to the media since all people expect it. Journalists are under pressure to prevent rumors and avoid misinformation and at the same time attempt to reach the frontline to broadcast news stories before other media companies.

Providing current information is a must when disaster or terrorist attacks occur, but there are long-term effects on children who view all media resources. Terror attacks in are horrific to both children and adults, but children suffer the long-term effects since television and wireless products are the tools of today's nonsocial outlets for people. Technology has added prolonged conditions to children. Children's protective shield is disrupted by media and can cause underlining development issues (Pynoos, Steinberg, and Wraith 1995). Children are watching the destruction of terrorism when people's homes are destroyed. In the same coverage children are killed, which viewers start assuming emotional thoughts of "what if," and speak of the matter as if they experienced the conditions firsthand. Add viewing experience with physical experience, and then the conditions multiply.

It is common when communities experience disaster or terrorist attacks to have a high rate of mental-health issues and acute stress disorders. Events experienced also lead to posttraumatic stress disorder, depression, and sleeping disorders (Balaban 2005). Children feel hopelessness as they continue to process media and terrorist attacks. Children are influenced by terrorism and violence they are surrounded by, such as domestic violence, gang activities, rape, and more. The media provides such connection daily.

Continuous media connection to violence like terrorism affects children by allowing intense exposure to situations. Children are not fully mature, and such media viewing or connection to devastation can disrupt daily routines, which scar children psychologically (Leavitt 1993). If a child has lost a family member in a terrorist attack or other traumatic event, viewing media coverage of the event can deepen the scars. There are short-term and long-term effects on people, especially children. I mention this since terrorism is an abnormal occurrence in normal populations. The majority of people that experience such intense events will show signs of acute stress.

The rationale of a child is not more mature than adults, so situations will seem greater than what occurred. Terrorism is geared toward a larger audience in order to convey a message from the terrorist organization. Children who experience such devastation may hate those who caused it and seek revenge throughout their lives. The media is capable of providing a great deal of options to keep people in touch with events. For children who have experienced a traumatic event first hand, exposure to media coverage causes children to suffer long-term affects due to constant reminders.

Both Homeland Security and terrorists will rely on the media. The media is expected to inform the public and maintain calmness in the delivery to prevent panic. Without the media, the public would not be able to connect with the government in order to identify that all precautions are being met to protect the American people. This is what Americans do not understand when they argue First Amendment rights. As years continue and terrorism becomes more common, there is a requirement for the media to provide information clearly, accurately, and efficiently. Journalism has a public service role that many abuse but Americans trust journalists when unexpected disaster or terrorist attacks occur.

Terrorism will continue to cause psychological trauma, especially when the public becomes complacent. Individuals and communities who expect terrorist acts to happen have a higher level of readiness, which allows for better reaction. Regardless of the readiness levels and trauma received due to terrorist attacks, children will have a long road to recovery. The media is the information train of the world and must practice due regard when publishing news, especially the news by means of continuous advancing technology, can trigger the past memories of people who mentally suffered from terrorist attacks.

If I was the boss for one day, my first implementations for all emergency services are mental health providers. There is much assistance provided for military war veterans, but our emergency service personnel are suffering equally, if not more.

In addition, if I were chief of a police agency, fire department, or emergency service squad I would have a dedicated journalist who climbed through the ranks of the department and appoint him or her with those very responsibilities so people see the good. Our police, fire, and EMS are under appreciated for the responsibilities they carry. It is rare to hear the good!

If you feel that the media has a powerful punch on society, wait until you read the next chapter on cyber terrorism. Technology is a hidden threat that takes advantage of people who rely heavily on computers and all technology alike.

Chapter 6

CAN SOCIETY BE AFFECTED BY CYBER TERRORISM?

GROWING TECHNOLOGY HAS created an increased frequency of cyber attacks due to the capabilities to access any source of information. This is a threat to any country's national infrastructure. There is no question that information technology will soon become the next arena of war between governments, which indicates that the security of such technology is required.

The cyber-attack in Estonia on April 27, 2007 affected both political and economic infrastructure. The Russians initiated the attacks because the Estonian government was preparing to move a Russian bronze soldier World War II memorial to another location, but the Russians believed that the memorial was to be removed completely (Shank 2011). The initial attack was against the Estonian president, prime minister, and parliament (Shank 2011). The attack was unsophisticated; it was identified by the United States Department of State as a cyber riot more than cyber war to harass the political ruling party of Estonia (Hollis 2008). Russian foreigners in Estonia provided capabilities to any person in the country who was willing to commit such cyber attacks (Hollis 2008). The denial-of-service attacks were sent out as spam by defacing official Estonian websites (Shank 2011). Local media in Estonia quickly accused Moscow of conducting the attacks, believing that Russia conducted the attacks due to the movement of the statue (Hollis 2008). In April 30, 2007, a more deliberate attack was conducted in Estonia, but the government network could not handle such an attack due to the size and intervals the attack was conducted (Hollis 2008). A few days later, other attacks were made on the banking industry in the country, causing tremendous monetary losses on international banking (Hollis 2008). The Estonian government requested assistance from the Northern Atlantic Treaty Organization (NATO); in response to the request, specialists in cyber security assisted Estonia to strengthen the security procedures already in place (Hollis 2008).

On August 8, 2008, Georgia launched military attacks against South Ossetia, and the press in the country was reporting the events as they unfolded (Hollis 2008). Russia deployed troops into South Ossetia. Soon afterward, the Georgian official website was defaced with numerous photos of Hitler followed by the server being closed by a denial of service; many other official government sites as well as banks were also attacked (Hollis 2008). On August 9, 2008, the president of Georgia, Mikheil Saakashvili, immediately blamed Russia for the cyber attack (Hollis 2008). United States officials believe that Russia may have been behind the attacks, but it is impossible to determine who conducted the attacks (Hollis 2008).

Whoever launched the attacks against Georgia did not shut the country down, because Georgia is not dependent on the Internet. What hurt the country more than cyber attacks was the physical use of Russian troops fighting in Georgia, but on August 12, 2008 the, European Union negotiated an agreement with the fighting countries to ceasefire (Hollis 2008). The Russian Troops were in Georgia as a result of the 1992 South Ossetia War between Georgians and Ossetians. The conflict resulted in Russian control. Understanding the history, the cyber attacks were hard to trace responsibility, but Russia may have been attacking Georgia to gain access to The United States since America supports Georgia in military training and provides weapons (Hollis 2008). Prior to this attack, Georgia was more in fear of physical occupation of Russia than cyber control. The attacks truly punched the country's infrastructure down and placed fear in Europe and United States. Google and neighboring countries were willing to strengthen Georgia's official government network, but Georgia did not accept and strengthened air defenses instead (Hollis 2008).

In 2006, there were many cases of United States government computer systems being hacked into by unknown sources in China (Krekel, n.a.). Before the Department of State was compromised, the United States Department of Commerce and United States Congressman Frank Wolf's office computer were hacked by unknown sources in China (Krekel, n.a.). In summer 2006, the Department of State was hit by a hacker who placed worms on computers for State Department employees to access through e-mail (Stewart 2009). The State Department conducted an investigation, and the trace of the attack revealed that desktop computers were tainted by a worm causing the computers to become part of a bot-network controlled by one hacker located in East Asia (Kamien 2006). The majority of the Department of State's infected computers were also in East Asia. The victims of the attack were State Department employees since their personal information and bank accounts were compromised (Buzzle Staff 2006).

The reason for such attacks is unknown, but it is suspected that it is as a result of the United States involvement in human rights issues in China. The attack proves that the Department of State has computer systems that can be easily accessed and need data-security programs to protect employees and American interests overseas. The State Department issued a memo to all employees to refrain from using any password-required source on desktop computers in workspaces until defense measures were established. It is unknown what protection measure was created to protect another intrusion.

These three scenarios of cyber terrorism and information warfare share some similarities yet also have differences. Both the attacks on Estonia and Georgia involved denial of service. Russia seems to have been behind attacks in both Estonia and possibly Georgia, and though it is not certain who the aggressors were in Georgia, both sets of attacks seem to have been politically motivated. It is possible that the attacks on the State Department in the East Asia Bureau were also politically motivated, but in this instance by someone in China. The State Department attack was different in that an individual who hacked into the State Department computers and infected them using a worm to target personal information and banking data initiated it. In the case of Georgia, banks were directly affected by attacks.

Based on this analysis, personal financial information and banking interests are vulnerable. Unknown people are conducting cyber attacks and groups due to the vulnerable software computers use to protect from such attacks. This makes it difficult to create defense mechanisms when hackers adapt to every new product developed that protects and operates computers. The best defense mechanisms from hackers are dependent on programmers of software (Cyber-attack Techniques and Defense Mechanisms 2002). Programmers of software need time to develop programs to withstand or prevent flaws and attacks of worms like malicious codes. This can prevent most attacks, but hackers understand buffer overflow that programs cannot defend from (Cyber-attack Techniques and Defense Mechanisms 2002). Once hackers are in the computers or servers, they start their campaign using a variety of malicious attacks for malicious reasons (Cyber-attack Techniques and Defense Mechanisms 2002). Just think when the United States infrastructures are threatened by cyber-attacks used by terrorist organizations?

When you understand a basic power that cyber terrorism has over society, it is more concerning at a domestic level. This threat can be as simple as identity theft to compromising a federal database. I will only discuss "the forgotten" railroad system. Without the railroads, America would suffer tremendously in the national and international infrastructure. The world depends on electronic sources, including the computer, which reach opportunities beyond human physical capability. The reach of the computer established the new wave of cyber space. This allowed for an easy world, but one that is easily compromised.

Before electronics, there was the railway. The railway was developed in 1830s (West and Miller) whereas the first computer was invented in the early 1930s (Nixodorf). The railroad was the first in building the American infrastructure that we see today, and it is still a required source and supplier. The railroad is vulnerable to imminent cyber attacks attributable to the advanced technology of computers. Such an attack will target information that could disrupt railway transportation and could lead to worse as it depends on the type of cargo being shipped. Cyber attacks will clearly allow terrorist organizations to operate more effectively and easily without being noticed. Attacks will harm innocent bystanders affected by such spiteful activity. The psychological effects of cyber terrorism attacks on the railway are endless as technology continues to grow.

Every day we are threatened from terrorism through the simplest forms of identification carried by all Americans. These are driver's licenses, library cards, and bankers or credit cards that are also used to verify identity (Kamien 2006). We can expect terrorist organizations to continue to seek out vulnerabilities and then attack. Some attacks are clearly out in the open, and you know when they are hitting you. Others are without warning or notice. Cyber terrorism is an example of a covert operation. (Kamien 2006). Computers are surveillance and target tools because of the large amounts of personal information are stored on them. Anyone who can access or remove a computer can retrieve information. If someone is able to install software on a computer system, they can turn the computer into a surveillance device or a system that can control the tracking systems of rails. Computers can be tapped by a number of methods, ranging from the installation of physical bugs or surveillance software to the remote interception of the radio transmissions generated by the normal operation of computers (Kamien 2006). Computers have the long-term effect psychologically as terrorist can access them in the same manner a reasonable person can.

Overseas attacks targeting mass-transit systems such as passenger rail have continued to be an interest by terrorist groups (NSD). Historically, many attacks overseas against mass transit and passenger rail systems were conducted to coincide with higher ridership periods (NSD). This is most likely because such attacks cause increased casualties and economic disruption and because they act as a practice for an action against Americans on American soil (NSD). The United States has a well-publicized increase of ridership, which can enhance the attraction of such public transportation as a target (Bullock and Coppola 2009). This leads to much potential for cyber attacks and physical terrorism attacks by use of insurgent-type tactics and for using illegally armed groups or criminals (NSD).

Areas controlled by insurgents and illegally armed groups or criminals, locations of mob activity, roads, railroads, trails, rivers, border crossings, and heavily populated areas are normally considered high-threat evasion environments. A train in motion is subject to cyber terrorism and physical terrorism. Individuals on trains must consider the possibility of being captured, since computers can reveal the seating arrangements of people on board the train. Terrorist groups and illegally armed groups or criminals can use people as a hostage tool in shutting down a stretch of rail so the train they capture is used as a blocking device for another attack (NSD). As a first move, isolated persons should attempt to establish contact with law enforcement, break visual contact with hostile elements, and move to a secure hiding site. If in a damaged rail car, people should move away for as long and as far as possible (NSD). Again, this is possible only if terrorist groups are using computers to track passenger seating and the direction of trains.

Rail schedules and routes are highly regular and predictable; they afford terrorists multiple opportunities to board and leave the train without arousing suspicion. The Internet world of cyberspace is appealing to terrorist. They can access information that pertains to their interests. Maps, weather, and population can be identified through the web. This can aid any terrorist group in their daily activity in identifying rail schedules, routes, and any location they wish to take action upon (Kamien 2006). The benefit that terrorists have in using cyberspace is 'they not being counterattacked'. Their identity can be masked, and their location can be hidden (Kamien 2006).

Terrorists' use of cyberspace will lead to a long-term security concern that the railroad could fall short in addressing, especially in today's economy. The railroad requires billions of dollars to operate. Just imagine how much one train is worth including cargo and passengers. A terrorist attack on a train that was going to a popular location would raise much press because of the destruction that would take place. It could incur thousands of casualties and cost billions of dollars in destroyed cargo, not including the recovery efforts. Trains move through environments where trucks and technology can't reach. This type of space provides adequate time and planning for any activity from cyber attack to physical terrorist attack to take place and alter the infrastructure of communities that require such assets. In addition, how do we or the emergency services, or United States government educate the American communities about this serious threat that most Americans access daily?

The new hazard associated with today's new threat is cyber terrorism. It is imperative to educate the public on this type of threat to reduce fear. Educating the public has been done in the past for traditional threats successfully (Bullock, Haddow, and Coppola 2009), but the technology world we live in limits the means to protect people and American infrastructure from cyber-intelligent people who wish to create havoc by a click of a button (Kamien 2006). Creating a public education program for this new threat will require a means of presentation and up-to-date information (Maura 2007). Cyber technology is a continuous animal of new updates; it will be a challenge in itself to remain vigilant of changes in efforts to prevent cyber attacks.

Terrorists have reached the capabilities of destroying information technology resources (Bullock and Coppola 2009). They are doing this to harm, coerce, or intimidate others in order to achieve their political or ideology goals (Bullock and Coppola 2009). As years continue passing us by, the severity of cyber terrorism increases. Information technology is the world's root of communication, business, and more (Maura 2007). The world relies on the computer daily while not understanding the threat of cyber terrorism (Maura 2007). More seriously, cyber terrorism can reach critical infrastructures, including military control mechanisms

(Bullock and Coppola 2009). This proves the capability terrorists have in constantly developing new and innovative ways to compromise the ever-more complex system the world relies on daily (Bullock and Coppola 2009). This is why an education program must be developed and publicized within communities.

Public education is a task of teaching people how to prevent cyber attacks from terrorists, one person cannot achieve this task, but it could by many who wish to be a partner in the education campaign (Barr, Koppel, and Reeves 2005). The campaign must be convincing to the people being educated. A single element teaching the public will not work. It is essential to have a partner in order to be successful (Barr, Koppel, and Reeves 2005). The campaign partner must be an expert in the field with resources already established (Barr, Koppel, and Reeves 2005). This will allow for a well-developed strategy in creating a public education program.

The strategy developed surrounds what the public consensus is pertaining to cyber terrorism. This will encourage more of the community to learn the dangers of this newest hazard. Once the strategy is developed, the campaign needs to develop and procure the material required. This will aid the education process. The material can consist of checklists, pamphlets, pocket guides, and even magnets. When the material is review and completed, the information must be presented to the community. This can be achieved, depending on groups and audiences, through newsletters, media, direct mail, and meeting groups. There could be cyber-attack education presentations at high schools, and the focus must be direct. Like everything in the world, this campaign will need evaluations to show improvements of the program so the community can continue to be intrigued and involved.

Just as important as how a community could be educated about cyber attacks, is the information that should be presented. An important beginning point would be how to prevent cyber attacks. This is known as Cyber Security Alert Programs for computers (Bullock and Coppola 2009). Nontechnical and technical people can use this program. Using this asset will make all updates available about the continuously changing cyber threat (Bullock and Coppola 2009). The community also needs information on resources and contact numbers for agencies or groups. This would consist of cyber response groups, local computer emergency readiness teams, and Internet links to information regarding the topic (Bullock and Coppola 2009). A good resource in educating the community is local college campuses. Colleges can develop or offer college-level classes or certification programs for preventing cyber terrorism. A continuous challenge is maintaining the curriculum to current threats and technology.

Terrorism will continue to challenge the reasonable person with new developed threats that cause destruction to society. Regardless of the terrorist organizations' ideology or political interest, communities must feel protected. The only means in providing protection is through community-education programs. Keeping fear from the hearts of the community is challenging, but recovering hundreds of years of infrastructure will be deemed impossible after being attacked through the computers (Kamien 2006). The community is America's only defense to cyber terrorism through well-organized community education programs. As you can see, this is a threat we cannot control once executed.

Another example of threats we cannot control will be mentioned in the next chapter; it is a scenario. The scenario displays complications all emergency responders from all levels experience due to a simple attack. It is my made-up scenario to elaborate the importance all emergency services at all levels of government have in protecting the homeland.

If I were a terrorist, I would live and plan operations in the United States of America. The reasonability given to the American people goes far beyond any county in the world, this would allow me to hide and fall into the realm of having the benefit of the doubt.

Chapter 7

WHAT IF THERE WAS A CHEMICAL ATTACK?

MOST AMERICANS DO not understand the simplicity of terrorism, especially when terrorists use random locations and materials already absorbed or established in communities around the world. Terrorism has a long history, but in 1996, Osama Bin Laden submitted declaration of war against Western Civilization in the name of all Muslims who believe in Allah (PBS 1996). This became threatening waters to navigate as allies of America and Americans working abroad had many concerns. Since 1996, there have been recorded attacks against American interests in the United States and American interests abroad. Infrastructure was the objective of the attacks more than individual targets. Infrastructure includes facilities, services, and installations needed for a community or society to function (The American Heritage Dictionary 2011). Under United States Code 42, Chapter 68, Subchapter 6B-5195C of 2001, critical infrastructure is defined as those "systems and assets, whether physical or virtual, so vital to the United States that the incapacitation or destruction of such systems and assets would have a debilitating impact on security, national economic security, national public health or safety, or any combination of those matters" (Legal Information Institute, website 2001).

For example, California has many military installations and power-supply plants. A terrorist might well think of a chemical attack of many locations in California. One location I want to address is the Marine

Corps Base Camp Pendleton and the San Onofre Nuclear Power Plant. This information is only a scenario I created so you can see how terrorists think. The scenario is not generated from any classified or unclassified information from either location. Again, this is my example to the reader of how terrorists think.

Both Camp Pendleton and San Onofre are on the Interstate-5 between Oceanside, California, and San Clemente, California, along the waterway, which has a rail system that operates through or along side both installations. These locations have potential to capture tourism, commuters, military, and public works by simple use of the mass transit system. Interstate-5 provides opportunity for intrusions due to the shipment of any type of chemicals that keeps the current American infrastructure running. Google the emergency response guidebook and notice what can be around you while you are driving, boating, or even commuting on a train. Both locations have no layered defense measures nearest the Interstate except a fence with barbed wire. There are police or security patrols for both locations, but it requires time to travel off installations to investigate unknown activity on the Interstate. This means that threat detection, public address, assessments, and response will be challenged when any terrorist attack is initiated from the Interstate or from a marine vessel. Not to mention, a chemical attack initiated in two areas on the Interstate or connected rail system would provide response issues for all first responders assigned to the local area due to chaos on the Interstate.

Here is something to consider, the San Onofre Nuclear Plant did offer tours before the complete shutdown. Any terrorist group planning an attack could have requested a tour and plan from what they observed. Another consideration to think about, an extremist or terrorist that displays a clean record could be hired on the security forces for either site mentioned, scary thought, but proves one of my theories regarding our "Current Fight Within".

Camp Pendleton has a police department and fire department with hazardous material response capability. Both are capable of responding to a terrorist attack, but combining attacks of the nuclear plant, highway, rail system, and military base would have memorable affects. If San Onefre Nuclear Power Plant and Camp Pendleton become targets of a chemical terrorist attack, both facilities would initiate the highest level of decontamination. Decontamination efforts are reserved for great numbers of victims who become exposed to harmful substances (Maniscalco and Christen 2011). Selected emergency medical services, police, and security personnel of both facilities, upon notification of a chemical attack, would require much assistance from local and federal authorities. Emergency decontamination is action taken by first responders to set up decontamination operations for victims in a field setting (Maniscalco and Christen 2011). This stage is good for rapid decontamination since the base fire department is equipped and structured for rapid response to hazardous- material contamination situations (Maniscalco and Christen 2011). Like many emergency response agencies in the United States, anything requiring first responding efforts beyond rapid decontamination will require support from many different agencies surrounding the incident.

If the nuclear site were still operating, look at this possibility: If an attack near the nuclear plant occurred, there will be energy operation concerns about the turbines and power shut down for 1.3 million residences connected to the site (Southern California Edison 2012). If the attack were successful at Camp Pendleton, would there be a mass evacuation of the people residing in the area of attack? Would environmental control be required since Camp Pendleton and shoreline has many restricted areas due to wild and marine life? In addition, both situations would cause cross contamination when initiated by terrorists. If chemicals dispersing from a tanker truck on the Interstate takes place, every commuter and metro train rider passing the initiation location would be exposed. This is just like the attacks on the World Trade Center when people used metro north to return to Connecticut or other locations, but they won't know they were exposed until miles down the road and would require self-admittance to a hospital or calls to 911.

Here's other consideration when situations like a chemical attack occur: As a first responder responding to a chemical attack, I understand the importance of having an incident-command center. The location of the command center would depend on weather conditions and contaminated areas. Specific to Camp Pendleton and the Nuclear site, the Federal Bureau of Investigation Field Office San Diego, Naval Criminal Investigative Services, Marine Criminal Investigative Division, Military Police Operations Command, Base Federal Fire Department, Oceanside Fire Department, Oceanside Police Department, San Clemente Fire Department, California Highway Patrol, Base Department of Environmental Control, United States Border Patrol and Homeland Security, United States Coast Guard, Railroad Authority, and Local Area Guard Forces from Camp Pendelton would respond to the incident. Each agency would have responsibilities ranging from communications to securing the Interstate and roadways. This situation could gain national press coverage, cause power outages for 1.3 million residences, possibly contaminate 3,200 to 7,000 people from the nuclear plant, Camp Pendleton, nearby residences, and daily commuters who could lose their lives, depending on the specific chemical, length of exposure, and the time symptoms were reported.

Regardless of the types of attacks conducted by terrorist organizations, terrorists have proven through time that soft targets are their preferred choice. Soft targets like Camp Pendleton, externally, not internally, and the San Onofre Nuclear Plant prove that much collaborative efforts from government with local sectors would be required to mitigate, respond, and recover from any terrorist attack. There have been many improvements to protect the nation from attacks, but looking at the obvious will not allow prevention of the unknown. Unknown soft targets do influence the impact an attack would have on tourism, commuters, military, and the public.

Terrorists live off the fear and emotions of victims, which drive their intent. If society doesn't allow terrorists to dominate lives through fear, terrorists will lose momentum.

Chapter 8

WHAT DOES TERRORISM MEAN TO IMMIGRATION ENFORCEMENT?

CHAPTER 7 MENTIONED the United States Border Patrol assisting in contamination efforts if a terrorist attack did take place, which is due to their checkpoint, located on Interstate-5 and immigration enforcement efforts within that area. Like many other areas of concern highlighted in this book and by the attacks on September 11, 2001, border security has become a priority. When discussing border security most people assume Mexico as the problem, but in truth, concern spreads to the United States air travel, ports, checkpoints on land, and land not in direct control of the Border Patrol or Homeland Security, or law enforcement agencies that protect communities near borders. When looking at the bigger picture of the United States entry points, there is great difficulty in security control. The security control of entry points became more pronounced immediately after the terrorist attacks in 11 September 2001, and proved the there were greater issues for many years to come.

When I analyze immigration enforcement issues in the United States, there are three areas that require sharpening to aid in antiterrorism operations: (1) Fraud, (2) Terrorism, and (3) Illegal Border-Crossing Activity.

(1) The current issue with fraud is dealing with passports. For example, 2010 had a rise of 100 counterfeit passports collected by federal border officials (Isackson 2010). The crackdown has been continuous and forces the hand of United States Congress to establish new policies to aid in enforcement efforts. As a result of such problems with fraud the Immigration Fraud Prevention Act of 2011. This act,

Amends the federal criminal code to subject to a fine, up to five years in prison, or both, a person who: (1) knowingly and falsely represents that he or she is an attorney or accredited representative authorized to represent aliens in immigration proceedings, including removal proceedings; or (2) knowingly executes an immigration-related scheme to defraud a person, or to receive money or anything of value from any person by false or fraudulent pretenses, representations, or promises. Amends the Immigration and Nationality Act to direct the Attorney General (DOJ) to: (1) compile and update a list of persons who have provided pro bono representation during the most recent 12-month period to aliens in removal proceedings, and (2) compile, update, and make available to the public a list of individuals, organizations, and practices determined to be prohibited in the provision of representation in immigration proceedings, including individuals that have been convicted of immigration fraud under provisions of this Act (Feinstein 2011).

(2) Terrorism is another concern, and border operations are an asset in preventing terrorism within the United States (Lamm 2002). The United States does have the watch list for countries that sponsor terrorism, but it is not sufficient given the recent "underwear" bombing attempts (Greenemeier 2012). Terrorism and immigration do go hand-in-hand; terrorists have the financial capability to make passports, use new identities, and pay people to cross the United States borders to conduct attacks (Lamm 2002). When there are borders as extensive as America's (2,000 miles in the south and 4,000 miles in the north) and there are only approximately 400 to 800 border patrol agents conducting policing operations, entry into the United States is likely (Lamm 2002). In addition to the expansive borders, the people who cross illegally find any available income. According to Lamm,

there are more chances that illegal immigrants would not become part of terrorist activity since immigrants are looking for better lifestyles for their families, but terrorist organizations make every effort to capitalize on this opportunity through large amounts of money directed toward recruitment (Lamm 2002).

(3) The miles of border not protected allow for illegal crossing activity. The United States border security is a challenge due to constant criminal activity. Criminals, including terrorists (DHS 2012). The majority of the illegal activity is the import or export of counterfeit goods and large amounts of cash. The cash is used toward the drug smuggling efforts or human trafficking (DHS 2012). Knowing these activities and main locations are very important for the border security efforts for the execution of law enforcement and antiterrorism (DHS 2012).

Examining state and local law enforcement agencies' authority to create and enforce their own immigration policies showed shocking results. The Department of Homeland Security, Immigration and Customs Enforcement allows state and local law-enforcement agencies to enforce and conduct operations under a joint Memorandum of Agreement (MOA). This MOA allows state and local agencies to receive delegated authority for immigration enforcement within their jurisdiction (ICE 2012). The MOAs established by DHS to local jurisdictions fall under a federal program call 287(g) Delegation of Authority. The 287(g) program can cause immigrants to avoid police, especially if they are victims of a crime (ICE 2012). In addition, this program would take regular policing away from the local community as it gains potential to create trust issues between community and law-enforcement officers. Local law-enforcement agencies can easily violate regulations that have changed due to lack of information. Immigration control takes place in a constantly changing environment. It requires one entity to enforce laws and regulations pertaining to immigration, which should be the different components dedicated to immigration within the US Department of Homeland Security.

The component of the US Department of Homeland Security that is responsible for immigration enforcement is Immigration and Customs Enforcement (ICE), which is the largest group of investigators (Nunez-Neto 2008). Their mission is the enforcement of federal immigration and customs laws. ICE can also provide security protection for facilities on federal property (Nunez-Neto 2008). Since ICE is part of the Department of Homeland Security, the primary focus of effort is dedicated to identifying vulnerabilities in national security and to preventing violations that can harm the United States. In addition to their duties and mission, the agency protects and serves the United States and the people of the United States through deterring and interdicting any threat that arises from travel of shipments, cargo, and people (Nunez-Neto 2008).

Another component in the Department of Homeland Security that is responsible for immigration enforcement is the Transportation Security Administration (TSA). TSA is responsible for the protection of United States air, land, and rail transportation systems. This ensures freedom of movement for people and commerce. The Aviation and Transportation Security Act (ATSA Public Law 107-71) created the TSA and included provisions that established a federal baggage-screener workforce, required checked baggage to be screened by explosives-detection systems, and significantly expanded the Federal Air Marshals Service (Nunez-Neto 2008). Another obligation that TSA is charged with is the security and protection of air cargo. It also oversees all security measures at airports, including "access to restricted areas, secure airport perimeters, and conduct background checks for airport personnel with access to secure areas, among other things" (Nunez-Neto 2008).

A stand-alone component of the Department of Homeland Security for immigration enforcement is the United States Coast Guard (Nunez-Neto 2008). It protects the public, the environment, and US "economic interests in maritime regions at the nation's ports and waterways, along the coast, and in international waters" (Nunez-Neto 2008). The United States Coast Guard is the lead federal agency for the "maritime component of homeland security, including port security"

(Nunez-Neto 2008). The Unites States Coast Guard is also responsible for "evaluating, boarding, and inspecting commercial ships as they approach United States waterways (Nunez-Neto 2008)."

The US Department of Homeland Security has many resources to conduct enforcement of immigration, and it should be able to adequately enforce immigration policy in the United States. There are two changes that might improve the ability of Homeland Security to enforce immigration policy. The first improvement should be dedicated to the southern border with similar technology as the northern border in order to open more entry and exit control points. Canadian and American officials have a program called NEXUS (DHS 2012). This program allows travelers that pass a background investigation to bypass routine inspections (DHS 2012). Each border has different concerns and operations, but this program will allow a more fluent crossing. In addition to this program, the second recommendation should be the adoption of US-VISIT at both borders. Airports have technology called US Visitor and Immigration Status Indication Technology (US-VISIT) to compare names of people coming into the country from a watch list (Electronic Privacy Information Center 2012).

There is no question that DHS, Border Patrol, and local law-enforcement agencies that enforce laws near or on the border have the largest mission in the United States as they attempt to keep the United States protected from fraud, terrorism, and smuggling. The September 11, 2001 terrorist attacks may have initiated overall concern toward all efforts mentioned, but border security is a growing problem with no easy approach. Mexico is not the only concern when discussing border security; it is an international realm that requires dialog in diplomatic affairs and information sharing with all agencies conducting immigration operations.

The freedom of America isn't the worlds to have, but available to those who dream the American Dream.

Chapter 9

WHY SHOULD WE BE CONCERNED WITH TERRORISM IN THE WORLD?

THE THREAT OF terrorism affects all communities both nationally and internationally. History has shown that no community is immune. Terrorism transcends all geographic and demographic boundaries, even Western Europe. All jurisdictions—suburban, urban, and rural— are at risk. This is has been extremely evident both domestically and abroad. On our own soil with the explosion at the Murrah Building and the tragic events on 9/11 we are excruciatingly aware of these kinds of attacks. In other countries, the cowardly attacks on the public have also proven that no one is immune. Terrorists have demonstrated their knowledge, ability, and capability to strike anywhere in the world. Biological and chemical terrorism have a much longer history than do explosives, as their use predates the use of gunpowder—as far back as the sixth century when drinking water in wells were poisoned and infected corpses were used a as tool of biological warfare.

The first event of chemical terrorism was described in the myth of Hercules and Hydra. This is only a myth, but it illustrates the psychological effect that people have from fear of such devastation. Hydra was a multi-headed creature that presented much danger to the populous of a small town of Lerna, Greece (Hoffman 2003). The creature had poisonous breath and also contaminated the drinking water of the Lerna Lake. This myth leads to reality in 300 B.C. when Greece polluted the enemy's drinking supplies with animal corpses (Harigel 2001). The Greeks used the same theory of chemical agents during the 431 BC Trojan War (Harigel 2001). These vicious attacks were due to political ideology aimed at dominating Europe. Greece was known for attempts to overthrow surrounding nations but with many failures. This leads to the early and late 1960s when the Greek government was ruled by military power (National Counter Terrorism Calendar 2011). In 1975 the November 17 or a.k.a. 17N terrorist organization formed in Greece (History of Greece 2002). It operated in Greece and was opposed to the politics of the government and performed attacks by use of explosives and hand guns against politicians and various United States embassy staff (National Counter Terrorism Calendar 2011). In 2000, a member of the November 17 terrorist organization assassinated the British defense attaché in a motorcycle drive-by shooting.

Similar to the November 17's politically motivated attacks, Rome had a terrorist group known as Judea Zealots that stem back to 52 BC (Twlushkin 1991). Zealots were known as dagger-men (Twlushkin 1991). Roman was an empire that believed that land was power. This attitude of the Roman Empire caused these Jerusalem freedom fighters to take up arms against Roman beliefs since Jerusalem was one of many countries that Rome wanted (Twlushkin 1991). The Zealots sharpened their daggers in water to cause a rusting residue and then rubbed the rusted blade on a dead corpse of animal or human remains (Twlushkin 1991). They did this in case the stabbing assassination alone wasn't effective but later caused a deadly infection in the intended target (Twlushkin 1991). Their targets would be any Roman politician or Jew that agreed with the occupation (Spindlove and Simonsen 2010, 53).

Zealots were soon identified as committing these attacks by officials, which later motivated the radical group to commit suicides in public. This eventually stopped the attacks against Roman politicians, but assassinations have continued in that region in modern-day politics. In 1978, Aldo Moro, president of the leading

Italian Christian Party, was working the compromise that would allow communists in the coalition government (Katz, n.a.). Moro was later kidnapped and assassinated by the Russian Red Brigade, a terrorist group that operated in the western European region (Katz, n.a.).

From 52 BC and beyond, the people or underground campaigns that kings authorized handled the majority of enforcement measures against terrible acts at a local level. In modern times, the United States and Great Britain have been targets interest of worldwide jihad against western civilization (Spindlove and Simonsen 2010, 194). Many European countries have been in a complacent state of mind until their major cities have become targets for suicide bombers (Spindlove and Simonsen 2010, 153). This explains why Greek authorities never made attempts to pursue or stop the November 17 Terrorist organization (Spindlove and Simonsen 2010, 153). Greece always had a laid-backed attitude regarding legal enforcement and international relations toward terrorism until after September 11, 2001.

Italy had a similar feeling and actions as Greece toward counterterrorism matters until the Madrid bombing (Spindlove and Simonsen 2010, 53). This situation coupled with September 11 terrorist attacks on the World Trade Center in New York City forced European nations to communicate or share information by establishing a multilateral relationship with each other (European Commission 2009). This relationship allowed the European nations to work together on counterterrorism efforts (European Commission 2009). The relationship also led to a Multi Legal Agreement Treaty with numerous of European countries and the United States (European Commission 2009), which Greece did not sign but Italy did. Nonetheless, Greece is determined to continue relations with the American ambassador and legal attachés to handle terrorism matters.

It is clear that the most important aspects of counterterrorism are the relationships between countries in Europe and North American communities. Police in both regions have developed outreach efforts by exchanging information about terrorists. This is important, as terrorist organizations declare war on the West, and the West has no other choice but to join together with policy makers, law-enforcement officials, and each other's judicial systems to effectively apprehend and prosecute terrorist. Like many areas of bilateral relationships, the fight against terrorism will need to continue and strengthening in order to effectively combat such aggression throughout the world, but do this without placing all efforts on the obvious.

There are other regions of the world other than America and Europe. Prior to the September 11, 2001 attacks in New York City and the Pentagon, terrorism was an isolated event in the United States that most Americans did not dwell on, since the attacks were not obvious.

The United States was not aware of the dangers of non-government organizations and radical Islam. Currently, the international community and the United States have become alert to the nature of terrorism movements and methods behind the ideology of terrorism. The direction that most politicians lean toward when the topic of terrorism arises is the influence of Middle Eastern countries, yet the majority of terrorism planning and operations are developed in Africa. Africa and the Middle East share beliefs and methods of terrorism, but also have distinctions. Both regions of the world have unique means to stem attacks globally, causing civilizations to crumble. Terrorists from both regions use assassinations or explosives that cause mass casualties to prove the power and movement capability terrorist groups have to cause fear and intimidation.

The terrorist groups that will be compared and contrasted are Qibla and al-Qaida. Qibla is located in Africa and al-Qaida is international but mostly in the Middle East. The first area of terrorist movements that Qibla and al-Qaida have in common is national or regional liberation to occupy an illegitimate territory. This is the most common motivation of terrorism and widespread in Third World countries. These groups can be categorized as rebel armies or extreme or radical anti-government groups (Moghadam 2011). The advantage of terrorists is the ability to blend into the populations of territories they occupy (Moghadam 2011). This leads to the locals financially supporting nongovernmental organizations for protection since local government cannot provide protection. This added protection measure guarantees opportunity for the terrorist groups to obtain weapons, receive sanctuary from surrounding communities, and receive resources of people or equipment from other territories that allow international influence (Moghadam 2011). What these groups will not participate in is collaborated efforts to overthrow nations that cause a change in culture and politics.

The second movement African and Middle Eastern terrorist groups share is an international aim toward destruction of social and political organizations. This is the most violent. Qibla conducted attacks in European countries against Latin Americans, Red Brigade affiliates, and Japanese Army Factions. Al-Qaida conducted attacks against America and American Interests abroad (Kamien 2006). Both groups are Muslim rooted and disagree with Western civilization beliefs, but al-Qaida is the only group of the two that had goals toward international liberation by reshaping the governments of certain countries (Kamien 2006). Both groups aim to project their power. They share international influence by occupying territories in nations that support terrorist groups. In this way, it may seem that nations are supporting terrorists, but these evil groups are also considered by some locals to be freedom fighters that fight against the nations' militaries since the political parties are unstable. Both groups share the freedom-fighter hat, but Qibla prefers to be a nongovernmental organization that claims to protect people's interests in local territories, such as fighting local drug lords and launching anti-western campaigns under the name "Muslims Against Global Oppression" (Or 2010, 19).

Qibla and al-Qaida have become very different in methods and motives due to their financial means (Kamien 2006). The majority of Africa is in a state of poverty where most Middle-Eastern countries are wealthy (Moghadam 2011). This explains why Qibla is more a nongovernmental organization than al-Qaida (Or 2010). Most poor states have rebellions or political violence that requires protection for the civilians of states. Poverty also leads to little to no education or career development, so joining a group of freedom fighters would be appealing. Recruits with potential will only become members if the leader of the group feels that the prospect can launder money and weapons and feels that the individual's beliefs are the same as the extremists (Or 2010). The leadership of the nongovernmental organizations come from poverty and bears much resentment toward Western civilization (Or 2010).

The resentment is shared with al-Qaida, as it may appear to be a war of Western civilization against Arab Muslims, due to the attacks carried out by Qibla and al-Qaida (Kamien 2006). This is not true, since most Muslims do not share the same belief. Today's war against terrorism is truly not a war against Muslims or Islam. Both African and Middle Eastern terrorist groups have conducted specific acts that portray an international agenda of their own ideology that threatens the international community and Western population. Both the groups in Africa and the Middle East are obvious threats that require Western and Muslim cooperation to battle such a destructive enemy which thrives off the territories of weak nations or hides within the communities that require protection that local government cannot provide.

The next chapters will discuss the obvious terrorism actions conducted. One was environmentally conducted but required the same or more effort by all emergency services to mitigate or save life.

Chapter 10

WHAT DOES A CASE STUDY PROVE?

DURING MY TIME in the Marine Corps, we used a saying, "Knowledge is Power" when studying material pertaining to the military. The same holds true, in my opinion, for the events discussed in this chapter. Case studies teach expectations of right and wrong. That is why all branches of the military and emergency services must conduct after action reviews to publish for other people to learn from mistakes and achievements. September 11, 2001 brought fear to the United States as al-Qaida demonstrated its willingness to rid the world of western civilization. Fear placed the Bush administration and our current administration in a proactive position to protect America more aggressively. These aggressive measures thwarted two different attacks al-Qaida planned from the country of Yemen. This proved that the airline system is still a target of opportunity for terrorism. The security of the United States has improved since the attacks of September 11, 2001, but operational changes and current policies need to be addressed to prevent or disrupt future attacks via aviation.

In order to understand how the attacks could occur, we must understand the enemy. We can only do this through the study of terrorism history and incidents. Al-Qaida is a self-organized group that reaches targets around the world. Its beliefs allegedly come directly from the Koran. Mixing the reading of the Koran and their strong conviction against western civilization has allowed members of the organization to become justified in their own ideology. This ideology has spanned to train and plan attacks in politically weakened states like Yemen. Al-Qaida members located in Yemen are known as al-Qaida in the Arab Peninsula (AQAP).

Yemen is a good location for terrorist organizations to train and plan attacks based on their ideology. The establishment of AQAP was new as of January 2009 (Kurczy 2010). The new organization under the name of al-Qaida located in Yemen just opened doors of opportunity of any outside terrorist entering Yemen to become affiliates with AQAP (Alexander, 2011). This is dangerous, and Yemen needs to put forth the same efforts the Saudi government has in order to prevent terrorism in their country. The Yemeni government has developed counterterrorism cooperation with the United States since the establishment of AQAP, but the political instability in and throughout different regions of Yemen has prevented means to eliminate terrorist locations or safe havens (Alexander 2011). Safe havens are locations that hide or protect individuals from the norm of daily lives of society for long durations and that allow time and space for planning and execution of extreme jihad ideology. The mastermind of AQAP is Anwar al-Aulaqi, who is now dead but also recruited outside terrorist using Yemen as a haven. He has deliberately trained the newly found recruits to hate America and the interests of America since 2009. One recruit he adopted was Umar Farouk Abdulmutallo. He trained him how to develop explosives and conduct suicide missions.

One mission that AQAP took responsibility for was the attempted detonation of underwear explosives worn by Umar Farouk Abdulmutallo. The attempt took place on a Northwest Airline Flight 253 that was boarded in Amsterdam to Detroit on December 25, 2009 (CBS 2010). After analyzing how this plot could occur, the weaknesses in homeland security were communicated between different federal agencies (Bryant, Murphy, and Zirulnick 2010). Umar's father communicated concern to American intelligence that his son was moving to Yemen and concerned with him joining a religious extremist group (Murphy 2010). The information from the father allowed the

United States government intelligence services to enter Umar into the Terrorist Identities Data-mart Environment, which came into effect after the signing of the Intelligence Reform and Terrorism Prevention Act of 2004 (Public Law 2004). This entry allowed his name to be viewed throughout the intelligence community, but the information provided did not meet the standards to be added to the watch list, the no-fly list, or the selectee list (Public Law 2004). This exposes the lack of information sharing between agencies. Department of State, Diplomatic Security, and the Central Intelligence Agency are responsible for foreign intelligence and travel. If information was accessible and made available on all systems established under the Intelligence Reform and Terrorism Prevention Act of 2004, Umar would have been detained in Amsterdam before boarding the plan for Detroit. When evaluating actions the US Department of Homeland Security should take to stop these attacks in the future will depend of the requirement of placing names of interest on all data systems. The current policy for placing names on a watch-list is based on levels of threat and concern addressed by the initial reporting. Operationally, the United States should make changes on the initial-reporting procedures that evaluate probability or likelihood that an individual is capable of conducting terrorist attacks. This should disrupt future attacks via aviation.

Another mission that AQAP took responsibility for was the foiled plot to deliver explosives to the United States (Joscelyn 2010). The explosives were placed in printer-ink cartridges and transported via a cargo plane from Yemen to Chicago on October 29, 2010 (Murphy 2010). AQAP intended to blow up the FedEx and UPS cargo planes over the Atlantic Ocean (Murphy 2010). According to Dan Murphy, "the bombs demonstrated a high level of sophistication and were likely to be lethal" (Murphy 2010). The plot could occur because Yemeni authorities lacked money and training (Joscelyn 2010). To support this statement, Fares al-Sanabani, the publisher of the *Yemen Observer* newspaper said, "You need equipment, you need training, you need know-how and you need intelligence. That's what Yemen is lacking and that's what Yemen wants" (Murphy 2010).

Dealing with this level of terrorism will require support and time. This attack was unique and did not compare to the underwear bomber (BBC 2012). This plot having been foiled illustrates that international intelligence has a responsibility toward preventing terrorism. When evaluating actions the US Department of Homeland Security should take to stop these attacks in the future rests solely on whether or not the United States allows DHS to be part of international relations.

Information sharing between agencies, such as CIA, DHS, and DOS, will improve training and communication opportunities for the Yemeni government. The United States is currently supplying $150 million dollars to aid in training Yemenis in counterterrorism, but there is worry from Yemeni analysts that this could create more bad than good (Bryant, Murphy, and Zirulnick 2010).

Fighting this level of terrorism will require the United States to address the ideology of such movements. If there is any change to policy to be made, it needs to address the transparency and facts behind such a threat. Until then, the United States will continue to engage in war that cannot be handled on a battlefield with such ideologically radical Islamists. Organizations like AQAP prove that simplicity and motives gain results, but take innocent lives. AQAP believes in using extremists who want to be known and receive credit for being part of a terrorism group when they are not. An example of this is the 1993 World Trade Bombings.

Terrorist attacks against the United States of America and its allies have become a serious threat to the very idea of civilized society. This makes terrorists and any groups or countries that support terrorist activity the enemy of the United States. What is difficult to understand is that the enemy is not one person—it is a single political regime. The regime is not a religious identity but an evil ideology that threatens the reasonability of everyday people in the world. The common man fears this enemy due to the premeditated, politically motivated violence used against noncombatants by subnational groups or clandestine agents. America's part in preventing terrorism became real in the 1990s just one year after President William Jeffery

Clinton was elected. President Clinton quickly became intelligent with the ways terrorists think and carry out their objectives, after the 1993 World Trade Center Bombing. America must feel safe, but the challenge for the newly elected administration was current technology, America's freedom of movement, and complacency, which the United States must change to deter such evil.

On February 26, 1993 at 12:17 in the unusually calm afternoon in New York City, an explosion occurred beneath the World Trade Center Twin Towers (Goldman 1995). The Towers consisted of an office space complex and the Vista International Hotel. The explosion resulted in the deaths of six people and approximately 1,040 people injured. The massive destruction to the garage area under the two buildings did not cause a collapse, but filled the Twin Towers with smoke that caused problems for the evacuations. A Ryder truck filled with explosives caused the destruction. This attack brought terrorism into perspective with concern for what form of attacks would take place in the future. The attack was politically motivated with efforts to disrupt the Western viewpoint of beliefs. The ideologies of terrorist groups truly range from far left to far right of the political spectrum, especially when many extreme forms come from far left, like Ramzi Ahmed Yousef (Goldman 1995).

The attack was not a suicide bombing, but methodically planned to employ explosives. According to a United States Army study, there are 109 versions of what terrorism is defined as (Falk and Morgenstern, page 3). This is one reason terrorism has been difficult to define. Different people view the same act and interpret it according to his or her experience; this doesn't exclude the prejudices and values of, either. The 1993 World Trade Center attack is considered terrorism according to the Federal Bureau of Investigations. The FBI definition of terrorism is "the unlawful use of force or violence against persons or property to intimidate or coerce a government, the civilian population, or any segment thereof, in furtherance of political or social objectives" (Maniscalco and Christen, page 214). While this is only one of many definitions of terrorism, by definition from the FBI, the 1993 bombing of the World Trade center was an act of terrorism.

The mastermind of the attack was Ramzi Ahmed Yousef, who was affiliated with extreme jihadist Palestinian Islamic Jihad (Falk and Morgenstern, page 55). Palestinian Islamic Jihad religion is Wahhabism (Falk and Morgenstern, page 42). The motive for the attack Ramzi Ahmed Yousef planned was religious ideology, yet to the world watching the news on the day of the attack, most people probably did not view such a deliberate action as connected to religion. In 1992, Ramzi Ahmed Yousef moved to America and pleaded political asylum (Mylroie 1995), one of many American freedoms he took advantage of, and located his affiliates in jihad, the affiliates were six other jihad extremist (Mylroie 1995). His affiliates were teaching religion on the side and smuggling cigarettes in order to make millions for Hezbollah (Emerson 2006, 217). The combination of terrorist organizations doubled the global network and influence of extreme jihadist (Viotti and Kauppi 2009, 3).

The amalgamation of members of al-Qaida and Hezbollah was cemented by their religious conviction to rid the world of Western evil. This being the motive of the attack, it was not executed following a religious ideology that uses males to conduct suicide attacks. Males were used to conduct the attack, but they did not give their lives for the cause. Regardless of religious success or not, the event identified a true threat that had full intentions to topple the twin towers (Mylroie 1995). The details behind the attack led to extremists entering the United States as immigrants, going to American schools, and marrying women who later converted to Islam (Mylroie 1995). Taking the time to build groups, the religion they facilitated from their residences was a powerful ideology that motivated people to bind together. In reality, religion and man have provided movements for many violent, unrestrained behaviors, such as the Crusades of the eleventh and twelfth centuries and Spanish Inquisition, which officially lasted until the mid-nineteenth century (Viotti and Kauppi, page 3). Today, Muslim fundamentalists have conducted movements in the Middle East, and Hezbollah has done the same in Lebanon, which established organizations like the Palestinian Islamic Jihad (Maniscalo and Christen, page 4). The history, the group, and the attack identified all motives of terrorism acts when the World Trade Centers where bombed in 1993.

The United States immediately initiated investigations that led to numerous groups of known terrorist organizations. The FBI located a Vehicle Identification Number (VIN) that belonged to the rental Ryder truck (YouTube 1993). Yousef fled America back to his home country to prevent capture. The FBI and New York City Police found evidence of plans for the 1993 attack and future attacks on American soil (Goldman 1995). Moreover, the FBI noticed characteristics associated with most terrorist groups. This group was an auxiliary cell in the Bronx (Goldman 1995). They also brought in supporters that paid for religious events, which made money. Indirect support was provided to their cause by al-Qaida and Hezbollah, which allowed the group to spend large amounts of cash for everything. Yousef and his six affiliates where oriented toward their cause and conducted training and acquired all material within the United States (Goldman 1995). The United States responded well to this situation and apprehended all suspects under United States federal law without the country going to war.

Bombing of the World Trade Center buildings in 1993 did not force the country into war, but it gave cause for a new fear of terrorist attacks against the United States of America and its allies. Law enforcement and emergency services have taken this threat very seriously and know that Western civilized society can be breached any time. Once attacked, the United States will make every effort to prosecute or pursue terrorists and any groups or countries that support terrorism. Prevention of terrorism has become a priority in the United States whether the terrorist are operating as one person or groups; it is a single political regime with evil intentions against humanity. In order for Americans to feel safe, its citizens must understand reporting requirements that assist law enforcement in terrorism prevention. Current technology, America's freedom of movement, and complacency are rights for all Americans to enjoy in the United States, but at what expense? America feeling safe is interesting when we have our own people conducting attacks deemed as terrorism, such as the Oklahoma City Bombings.

The Oklahoma City bombings clearly demonstrated the threat of terrorism in the United States domestic territory, especially from one of their own citizens. Lone actors of terrorism like Timothy McVeigh have caused fear in people for many years to come due to his devastating attack on an unlikely small southwest location. A hundred sixty-eight people lost their lives to this attack (United States Department of Justice 2000). Nineteen of the casualties were children in the daycare center near the top floor (United States Department of Justice 2000). Timothy McVeigh most likely selected this target because of his high level of anger against the United States government from his military experience in Desert Shield (United States Department of Justice 2000). His efforts were seamless in this heinous act since the target location was available. His actions by attacking the federal building represented a new phase in the development of emergency management (United States Department of Justice 2000).

Emergency preparedness for terrorism events became a concern as agencies battled about who is in charge of terrorism incidents: the Federal Bureau of Investigations or local jurisdictions. What took place on April 19, 1995 did change law enforcement view on antiterrorism matters. The response to the incident also proved difficult for combined agencies. The difficulty of response to any terrorism will depend on size of departments and resources available. Most agencies do not receive training in terrorism response (Oklahoma Department of Civil Emergency Management 1995).

Government agencies rely heavily on communications when disaster strikes. There were two means of communication at the scene during the recovery efforts: one was on-scene communication between all emergency responders and volunteers, and the second was public officials communicating to the community regarding the occurrence via the media (Oklahoma Department of Civil Emergency Management 1995). On-scene communication was handled by the incident command center. The command center only had the frequencies of local and mutual aid responders, not those of the volunteer groups that responded from all over the country and state of Oklahoma, which is understandable (Oklahoma Department of Civil Emergency Management 1995). Since many different agencies were working the site, they used their own radio equipment that led to communications of pertinent information being missed. There was not enough communication equipment for all responders, especially after the police department directed that the command center would use the police frequency only while operating at the scene (Oklahoma Department of Civil Emergency Management 1995). Responders also used cell phone, but AT&T was not an effective service and dropped many calls (Oklahoma Department of Civil Emergency Management 1995). The cell service contributed too much information being translated inaccurately by the media when chief officers of the fire department and police department attempted contact (Oklahoma Department of Civil Emergency Management 1995) but was not their primary focus since there was no person from the command center assigned as the public-affairs officer (FEMA 2011).

Public officials did not expect the outcome local and national media would have. In reality, most people rely on the news to receive information directly. The media broadcast any information they captured without filtering. The media took advantage of not being required to check into a public affairs officer and made several attempts to access the restricted area (Oklahoma Department of Civil Emergency Management 1995). This caused the command center to take rescue workers from the site and reassign them to controlling the media at entrée points (Oklahoma Department of Civil Emergency Management 1995). It was important that the media did not collect information or video of the injured and dead; this would cause more concerns of viewers as they worry about those they love that may have been at the site.

All wounded were cared for by the local Emergency Response Service (EMS). When EMS received the first 911 calls, dispatch sent one ambulance to respond (Larson, Metzger, and Cahn 2004). Once the dispatched ambulance was on scene, the EMTs informed dispatch that they needed more assistance (Larson, Metzger, and Cahn 2004). With no hesitation, seven more ambulances and twenty-four EMTs were rendering assistance within ten minutes (Larson, Metzger, and Cahn 2004). EMS established dispatch coordination at the site (Larson, Metzger, and Cahn 2004).

In addition to the dispatch coordinator, EMS also assigned a transportation coordinator (Larson, Metzger, and Cahn 2004). The transportation coordinator's primary responsibility was to keep track of available beds at hospitals and coordinate transportation of critical injured (Larson, Metzger, and Cahn 2004). Patients were classified in two categories. Category One was assigned to people with severe injuries that required immediate medical attention (Larson, Metzger, and Cahn 2004). Category Zero was assigned to remaining people, the dead or walking wounded (Larson, Metzger, and Cahn 2004). All walking wounded were treated at the site. One hour into medical operations, 50 ambulances arrived on scene and 139 patients were transported, but several other victims went directly to the hospitals from the site (Larson, Metzger, and Cahn 2004). This caused EMS to establish a local, onsite triage center. The EMS had many challenges during the operation; there were a couple of bomb scares announced, which halted emergency care until site was deemed safe to continue work.

Other safety challenges came upon the first responders regarding supplies and donations. The attacks of the federal building brought much media and volunteers since it was the first major disaster of this type in the United States (Cook 1995). This proved that there was a lack of training by local government agencies in the handling of donations, volunteers, and media. Media captured any moment to broadcast information to the community, which led to abundant of supplies being donated when there were adequate supplies for the job, due to the media over hearing an emergency operator needing gloves. Local emergency responders became overwhelmed in operations by the ill-tracked supplies and volunteers (Cook 1995). When dealing with volunteers and supplies, it becomes a nightmare for logistic operations as to what can be used and stored.

Two areas that benefited the operations were the multiagency coordination center and the incident-command center (Oklahoma Department of Civil Emergency Management 1995). The local multiagency coordination center had good working relations between numerous agencies at the scene, which led to the rescue efforts being streamlined. The incident-command center employed immediately once the first responding units deemed incident as a disaster (Larson, Metzger, and Cahn 2004). Local leaders came together to manage all personnel and to develop operational planning toward rescue efforts.

There are many actions that agencies could have done better surround communication, responsibility, and accountability (Oklahoma Department of Civil Emergency Management 1995). Communication on the radio or through cell phones did affect operations on the ground. During 1990, Federal Emergency Management Agency developed a communication capability that works during numerous natural disasters and response to bombings like the Murrah Federal Office Building (Oklahoma Department of Civil Emergency Management 1995). This system was being used at the site and proved to work effectively, but there was much confusing due to the many federal agencies pushing their weight around, which leads to responsibility (Cook 1995). This identifies that the federal response mechanism further complicates intergovernmental incidents and allowed communication to become an issue.

Federal agencies need to assist local leaders in the local multiagency coordination center, not place change to plans of operations without the command post knowing (Oklahoma Department of Civil Emergency Management 1995). The Federal Emergency Management Agency personnel coordinated with the local fire department, police department, and other government agencies on scene. Such coordination was necessary due to the efforts involved with the stabilization of the partially collapsed structure. The condition of the structure forced rescue and recovery effort to search in tight places, high-angles rescue, destroying concrete, and removal of all hazardous material that emergency service personnel came in contact with. This lead to who was not checking into the local fire department, police department, and other government agencies on scene, meaning emergency response and recovery to such disaster revealed concerns in identity management capabilities at all levels of government.

Oklahoma City police established perimeter control two hours after the explosion (Oklahoma Department of Civil Emergency Management 1995). In addition, the police department also set up their identification equipment so they could issue identification badges to all responding and relief personnel (Oklahoma Department of Civil Emergency Management 1995), which took two hours to make the badge for each person (Cook 1995). The identification process did not last long due to lack of supplies to service the massive numbers of emergency responders. It shouldn't take hours to process responding and recovery personnel during a tragedy. The local Secret Service Field Office setup a similar process once the Oklahoma City Police Department couldn't support such demands (Oklahoma Department of Civil Emergency Management 1995). This type of deficiency is a major concern regarding terrorism response, but the Federal Emergency Management Agency Mutual Aid and Resource Management Initiative doesn't specify guidelines to follow regarding Identification Management at scenes, Government SMART Card Handbook (GSA 2004).

Identification systems are important to responders and recovery personnel. The system allows for assignments to be issued and supervised and prevents confusion in the command center. Having no identification system or a system that changes daily would ultimately lead to emergency-service personnel being discouraged from rendering aid. In addition to the on-scene identification system, issuing of credentials to emergency service personnel became tedious. Every time workers who had been at the site several times arrived on scene, they had to show paperwork, department credentials, and have all equipment inspected by the Oklahoma City Police (Oklahoma Department of Civil Emergency Management 1995). All persons who went through initial screening should not have to go through the same rigors each time, but have a pass that is scanned which would allow access so members could report to the command center and receive new orders or continue working their specialty at the scene. Many of the volunteers who had specialties in recovery efforts and rescue operations had their laptops and other required tools confiscated by the police department at screening points when the same equipment the day prior was on scene (Oklahoma Department of Civil Emergency Management 1995). This is an example of how the investigation could have been difficult.

To summarize the situation, a Rider rental truck massively exploded in the front parking area of the federal building in the downtown portion of Oklahoma City. The explosives used by Timothy McVeigh, the bomber, were 4,800 pounds of Ammonium Nitrate mixed in oil. The explosives were loaded into a Rider rental truck. Not including the dead, there were 674 four people injured. The building was a total loss and several buildings in the downtown area were severely damaged. Rescue efforts went for sixteen days and had many resources (Oklahoma Department of Civil Emergency Management 1995), to include eleven Federal Emergency Management Agency's urban search and rescue teams, which came from across the country to assist the local and state officials in searching the destruction for survivors and bodies of those who perished in Timothy McVeigh's evil act (Cook 1995).

The explosion partially collapsed the building up to all nine floors. The construction of the building was twenty years old. This raised concerns to the fire department when they entered the building. They were unsure that the building would support weight of remaining structure (Oklahoma Department of Civil Emergency Management 1995). Communication was tough due to the many different agency involvement, but overall response to the attack went well.

Another situation that exemplifies great difficulty with emergency response to disaster equivalent to terrorism is environmental threats. There is no better case of such threat than Hurricane Katrina.

On the morning of August 29, 2005, Hurricane Katrina came from the Gulf Coast and swept through New Orleans, Louisiana. The storm itself did not threaten life, property, public health and safety as much as the break of the levies that normally keep the below-sea-level city safe. New Orleans has experienced many hurricanes. Hurricane Katrina did not seem different; people were prepared for the hurricane and the federal government was prepared to assist New Orleans in hurricane response. Government officials did not expect the worst: the levies breaking, which caused massive flooding. This incident made all authorities look to the next level of government for assistance.

This disaster caused questions to bloom regarding the specifics of state and local government authority to render aid. The public screamed for assistance and the government reacted slowly, most likely due to the shock settling from the levies breaking. The incident proved that the state required clarity of their authority and identify how the state was going to use the authority to implement plans, procedures, and delegation of tasks in emergency operations. The clarity of authority is mentioned clearly in the state constitution (US House of Representatives). The Louisiana Homeland Security and Emergency Assistance and Disaster Act is in the state constitution. It empowers the governor to address emergencies and disasters, including situations that cause floods, and evacuations (Proclamation).

Three days before Hurricane Katrina fell on New Orleans, Louisiana Governor Kathleen Blanco declared a state of emergency. After the declaration, practice of "Evacuation Plans" in the southern part of Louisiana differed from the governor's powers. Parishes under the evacuation plan have the authority to issue voluntary or mandatory orders within that parish community, not the governor (Proclamation). The southern Louisiana evacuation plan had three phases: (1) precautionary, (2) recommended, and

(3) mandatory. Risk-area parishes only used state authorities in a supporting role. This did not include a contraflow plan, however; if local governments failed to take action, the state could have overridden if proclamations were prepared. Either way, it is difficult to determine whether the governor or the parishes ordered complete evacuation (Proclamation). This inconsistency of authority proved true when aerial footage showed numerous buses under water due to buses being used for an evacuation that came from an unknown source of authority.

The Louisiana Disaster Act authorizes the governor to use any available resource reasonable to handle an emergency and allow communities to cope with such a disaster (US House of Representatives). These resources are the performance of emergency services, facilitating medical care, use of private property, use of public transportation, government-owned vehicles, and vehicles used by volunteer groups (US House of Representatives). The use of resources depends on phases of the emergency plan being executed. The precautionary phase alerts emergency employees and starts the stage in reviewing the evacuation procedures. This means establishing contact with special facilities in efforts to prepare for the plan of execution and advising all transportation to implement the public transportation plan. These tools can only be supported by the state, but require risk area parishes to be responsible. Again, this can cause confusion on who has overall authority. Risk area parish declarations mention that the state will assist when assets are not available, but the state has no way of identifying such need unless introduced in a proclamation. On August 31, 2005, the governor issued an executive order to provide transportation assets to Louisiana Homeland Security and Emergency Preparedness.

Assumptions by both the state and parish communities caused many questions when evaluating the operational capability of assets, with due regard of the evacuation, or any condition of such magnitude (Louisiana Office of the Governor). Only the governor can declare state of emergency and evacuation, (Louisiana Office of the Governor), yet the Louisiana Emergency Action Plan shows no clarification of how to implement authority and guidance of who exercises the authority. Unfortunately, both state and local governments in Louisiana failed to remember the levies that protect New Orleans when planning for response to catastrophe. It is not recommended to reverse authority from original plans and procedures in the midst of a disaster since it can cause chaos, but the emergency plan during Hurricane Katrina resulted in confusion of decision makers who had an opportunity to plan in advance. Authority is devised under effectiveness of government officials. If state government is willing to take responsibility, then a plan will be operational, but government must ensure training and education of elected officials, emergency responders, emergency planners, and those in the private sector.

To be effective as a manager, it is important to be prepared for any question that pertains to emergency preparedness. The book *It's OKAY to be the Boss*, identifies that checklists aid managers toward success. Subcommittees on the Homeland Security and Emergency Management created a checklist. This was created for the local government attorneys to prepare for possible disaster. As a good tool of reference, it provides a detailed guide for state and local governments to assess and implement their applicable legal authorities. This same checklist developed by the subcommittees was offered to public officials and local governments to prepare for disaster conditions, and included training of all people involved in disaster preparedness (Abbott).

Hurricane Katrina was well prepared for by Louisiana. It was lack of planning for the bigger picture that authorities failed to identify as a risk factor. During and after the incident, the Louisiana governor and the state's people wanted answers from the United States government on why they did not respond quickly enough. The answer is simple: Federal Emergency Management Agency was prepared for the hurricane, not the flooding. The United States government, through the Homeland Security Act of 2002, paid the State of Louisiana money each year to prevent flooding condition, since such a disaster requires more capability. The prevention money was required to keep the levies maintained and built upon, since the City of New Orleans is below sea level and flooding occurs if levies are broken. People in Louisiana did not die from the hurricane; the death toll was from the flooding condition that neither state government nor federal government could prepare for.

Capabilities identified prior to a manmade, or natural disasters are essential to making effective plans, just like an accepted antiterrorism program. Emergency management programs and antiterrorism programs share the same intent, but the intent of either was missed prior to Hurricane Katrina. The capability was identified, but appropriate actions were not taken when the timing was right.

Chapter 11

WHAT IS ANTITERRORISM IN THE UNITED STATES?

THE WAR ON terrorism has proven to be a challenge, but protecting the United States Infrastructure will continue as a top priority. Antiterrorism tactics have evolved as terrorist attacks have changed and become more deadly throughout history. The strategies today that aid antiterrorism would not be in existence if the attacks did not occur on September 11, 2001. This tragedy taught the United States that terrorism is indiscriminate in actions against the nation and innocent people. This threat requires the American government to initiate proactive antiterrorism measures. These measures can only be managed at a local level with support of federal capabilities. Together, local and federal authorities at public, government, and military levels can have a program that has tactics and organization that allows society to be alert to the threat of terrorism. Moreover, it requires Americans to be aware of each other's surroundings to ensure the safety of their families and the United States as a whole. If the United States slacks in preventing terrorism, the country is at risk for terrorism to become a way of life in America as our Founding Fathers feared (Ellis 2007). The antiterrorism effort will examine terrorism more thoroughly with political support that allows police and military to work together in measures that deter, mitigate, and prevent terrorist attacks. Both entities together will achieve this through information sharing.

Information sharing and understanding terrorism cannot occur without examining terrorist threat. First, terrorism must be defined. The United States Patriot Act states that terrorism is not classified as a crime until violence is used against people or property that threatens government political positions (Sensenbrenner 2002). This supports the Federal Bureau of Investigation definition, "Terrorism is violence or threat of violence, calculated to create an atmosphere of fear and alarm" (Federal Bureau of Investigations website 2005). Terrorism is true violence or threat of violence directed against human rights. Regardless of culture, a terrorist can be any person that can hide within population. When the time is right for actions to be used against political parties or national freedoms, fear is created. This fear can be easily exaggerated by portraying nongovernmental organizations, freedom fighters, or cell-operated terror groups as stronger than they are (Waugh 1983). Strong or weak, the actions of these organizations have a long-term psychological effect on society and they attempt to intimidate governments to comply with their wishes (Waugh 1983).

This type of provocation caused by terrorist groups has a supporting history. There are numerous examples of politically driven terrorism throughout history. The violence became well known in 1793 during the French Revolution when terrorism was used as a tool by the French state representatives (Ansart, n.a). In 1901, an anarchist shot and killed William McKinley, the twenty-fifth president of the United States (Miller Center 2011). In more recent history, states like Iran that support terrorism have a long history in aiding nongovernmental organizations (Bruno 2011). This history reveals organizations and tactics used against targets. Examples of terrorism acts conducted by clandestine nongovernment state actors include the incident on December 17, 1981 when terrorists of the Italian Red Brigades kidnapped US Army Brigadier General James Dozier from his residence in Verona, Italy (Phillips 2002). Red Brigade terrorists decided Brigadier General Dozier was a desirable target because he was a senior US official and his routines made it possible to plan an attack (Phillips 2002). Another example took place in Greece on November 15, 1983, when terrorists of the November 17 Organization on a motorcycle overtook Captain George Tsantes in his US Embassy sedan and shot him (Department of State 1985). This attack on a US security assistance officer signaled a new terror campaign against US military bases in Greece (Department of State 1985).

Americans' safety is threatened by terrorist actions conducted by clandestine, nongovernmental, state actors that target United States interests (Terrorism Research, n.a.). Many of the actors are affiliated with countries like Iran, since Iran supports groups that threaten American civilization (Bruno 2011). In addition to clandestine nongovernmental actors threatening the American way of life, diplomacy is also threatened. Iran has been seeking nuclear control, which causes poor dialog with American politicians (Bruno 2011). Poor collaboration with Iran forces world leaders to make moral and ethical choices that prevent future disasters. If decisions are not made and actions against such threats are not executed more clandestine nongovernmental state actors will conduct terrorism attacks with Iranian support (Bruno 2011).

Many modern terrorism organizations state that their actions are based on religious beliefs. On October 23, 1983, a large truck crashed the barricade of the US Marine compound at the Beirut International Airport and penetrated the entrance to the Marine Battalion Landing Team Headquarters (HQBLT) building and exploded, killing twenty-four people (Ziegler 1998). As fighting among Lebanese factions intensified, US forces provided support to the Lebanese armed forces. The Islamic Jihad Organization made the attack with Iranian and Syrian sponsorship (Ziegler 1998).

Attacks against United States interests connected to extreme Islamist groups include the one on June 25, 1996 when terrorists exploded a massive truck bomb outside the Khobar Towers housing complex in Dhahran, Saudi Arabia, killing nineteen US service members, and injuring hundreds of other service members and Saudis (Ziegler 1998). The bomb was huge, estimated at nearly 20,000 pounds (Ziegler 1998). Terrorists can mount devastating attacks anywhere, so teamwork and vigilance are essential. Unfortunately, unit security measures did not prevent this attack, but alert guards saved many lives. Guards saw a truck park near the fence and its occupants drive away in another car. They immediately started an evacuation, but the bomb detonated only four minutes later (Lemoine 2007).

The Department of Defense investigated the attack and implemented new programs to promote the safety of US forces worldwide known as Antiterrorism Force Protection (Lemoine 2007). On military bases throughout the world, there is a military service member that that carries the responsibility as an antiterrorism officer. Peacetime or wartime, this person makes bases and areas of operation hard targets for terrorist organizations. The antiterrorism specialist implementing antiterrorism means to assist in making decisions on mitigation, security measures, and deterrence is essential, but challenges in this area require antiterrorism measures to adapt to various kinds of threats and vulnerabilities. Threats and vulnerabilities can be controlled through risk management, which is a reliable approach to identify techniques and exposures. The antiterrorism measures used for military installations soon became the responsibility aboard naval and army ships. On October 12, 2000, terrorists attacked the Arleigh Burke Class Destroyer USS Cole (DDG 67) during refueling in Aden Harbor, Yemen (Lemoine 2007). Two individuals maneuvered a thirty-five-foot craft laden with explosives to the port side of the Cole and detonated it (Lemoine 2007). The blast ripped a thirty-two by thirty-six-foot hole, killing seventeen and injuring thirty-nine crewmembers. Heroic efforts by the crew saved the ship. The attackers showed no sign of hostile intent before the explosion and crewmembers believed the craft was involved in routine harbor activities. In fact, the attackers smiled and waved in a friendly manner as they maneuvered their craft alongside the USS Cole (Lemoine 2007).

The situation with the USS Cole caused the military to place antiterrorism measures within the Army Maritime Preposition Shipping Units and Naval Fleet deployment programs. Each unit that deploys oversea, regardless if it is non-combat or combat operation, has an antiterrorism officer assigned by the commanding officer of deploying units. The antiterrorism officer will serve the same purpose as an installation-assigned specialist in antiterrorism. Peacetime or wartime, this person makes deploying units a hard target.

Terrorists will not risk the effort to attack a hard target when weaker targets can produce more outcomes toward their cause. An example of this is September 11, 2001, when a hijacked passenger jet, American Airlines Flight 11 out of Boston, crashed into the north tower of the World Trade Center. A second hijacked airliner, United Airlines Flight 175 from Boston, crashed into the Trade Center south tower. Subsequently, both towers of the World Trade Center collapsed as burning jet fuel melted steel girders. Yet another hijacked airliner, American Airlines Flight 77, crashed into the Pentagon, and United Airlines Flight 93, crashed in Somerset County, Pennsylvania, after passengers struggled with hijackers (Lemoine 2007).

These events shook the world as many Islamic cultures celebrated the attacks against Western civilization. The attacks brought a new approach to antiterrorism. One of the first methods was a relaxed domestic spying guideline that many American frowned upon due to civil liberty questions (US Government Accountability Office 2002). Another method used was the detention of 1,200 middle easterners for immigration violations (US Government Accountability Office 2002). The third method was by the Department of Defense when there was a noticeable difference on the manner military branches conducted antiterrorism. The Department of Defense mandated the need to issue a strategic plan on 15 June of 2004 and established a new management framework for antiterrorism under Department of Defense Directive 2000.12.

The methodology behind antiterrorism that organizations utilize: deterrence, detection, delay, defense, mitigation, and recovery from a terrorist attack, thereby reducing the vulnerability of American citizens (Kamien 2006). Antiterrorism is the leading concept of defensive measures taken to reduce vulnerabilities with the definition of whom and what is being protected (Kamien 2006). America has evolved where American citizens may encounter a wide variety of hazardous conditions in today's domestic environment. These conditions may exist under a wide variety of circumstances to include hazardous materials or terrorism-related situations. Having an understanding of the processes to remove or decrease the effects of terrorism is the motivation for all Americans to learn and practice. It is crucial that American families, entrepreneurs and their employees, and equipment and facilities of critical infrastructure be prepared at all levels to implement antiterrorism measures and make the appropriate decisions to protect themselves and the United States. The emergency services at all levels will hold the ultimate responsibility that entails elevating the awareness, security, and response capabilities of all agencies required to handle such devastation.

The emergency services and all agencies at all levels currently have the tools to support the methodology of antiterrorism. According to PBS *Frontline*, here are some of the tools available, but not limited to: (1) the Uniting and Strengthening America by Providing Appropriate Tools Required to Interrupt and Obstruct Terrorism Act of 2001; (2) Homeland Security Presidential Directive Number 2; (3) National Commission on Terrorist Attacks upon the United States 107-306; (4) Intelligence Reform and Terrorism Prevention Act of 2004; (5) Foreign Intelligence Surveillance Act; (6) National Incident Management and National Framework of Emergency Response; (7) Integrated Public Alert and Warning Systems; (8) Electric Communications Privacy Act; and (9) Wire Tapping Title III.

These are tools that aid in critical analysis of having an effective antiterrorism program that solidifies deterrence, detection, delay, defense, mitigation, and recovery from a terrorist attack, thereby reducing the vulnerability of American citizens. In order to conduct rigorous antiterrorism, public officials and emergency managers at a local level need to have a sound antiterrorism plan. Every plan needs to be tested and validated by regular assessments that encourage training and exercise for all emergency responders and citizens. This type of planning will form the base of physical security, operational response and recovery, shared intelligence between agencies at all levels, information gathering that counters terrorism, and security programs for private corporations and businesses (Kamien 2006).

When emergency services from all levels plan effectively, it will lead to identifying the likely consequence of an incident, pointing out important questions and determining whether or not any reasonable expenditure of resources can prevent the consequences (Kamien 2006). It is a priority of local authorities with political support to identify the sum of all threats through vulnerability assessment and critical assessments (Kamien 2006). Together, local officials will be able to mitigate the risks.

There are numerous ways to improve the effectiveness of antiterrorism efforts. Local officials tend to move away from antiterrorism practices or even fail to speak of antiterrorism. While the topic may frighten people, discussions about terrorism, its effect on society, and how to prevent it are essential. Until public officials feel comfortable with the organization and tactics of antiterrorism, it will remain a challenge for emergency responders to respond and recover from major attacks conducted by terrorists. In aspects of public service, there are integrated means available to employ antiterrorism tactics that could improve effectiveness to achieve its goals.

One agency that individual state governments in the United States can implement is the Department of Homeland Security. This development would support the mission of the United States Department of Homeland Security but at a state level. This would also provide individual states opportunity to qualify for federal funding that supports antiterrorism and emergency management of disasters. Emergency management is mostly an individual county concern within individual states, but Homeland Security efforts can force efforts of all agencies to share information and resources. Public safety doesn't have the manpower and tools available to accomplish proactive antiterrorism and emergency management.

If each state has a Department of Homeland Security they can use this newly establish agency to augment shortfalls in law enforcement and incident command systems. Law enforcement participation is essential since state infrastructures are not being secured or patrolled as routinely as needed. All law enforcement agencies are overwhelmed with domestic response, which relates to reactive operations. These operations are time consuming and prevent state police, county sheriffs, municipal police, city police, and private police from conducting antiterrorism measures. The individual states' departments of homeland security could assist all law-enforcement agencies by patrolling critical infrastructures, rail systems, maritime, and arterial roadways to conduct traffic management. The number-one counterterrorism measure for law enforcement is a simple traffic stop. Just simple images of traffic stops and a uniformed officer near a critical infrastructure could change the plans of a terrorist.

One more tactic organizations could implement to improve their effectiveness in antiterrorism is to provide special training and support to first responders to protect communities from the effects of terrorism. First responders lack assistance and information about threats in their jurisdictions. Terrorists' destructive ability has been seen through the use of explosives. Emergency service first responders must be prepared to handle secondary devices or other threats while maintaining the initial responder's ability to control the scene and save lives. In addition, procedures for the Department of Homeland Security at state level, local fire, police, and ambulance services should set up terrorism liaison officers or antiterrorism officers to concentrate on the perimeter and beyond of emergency scenes for unusual activity characterized as possible terrorism surveillance. This allows for more citizens to be hired protecting those that serve communities in emergency civil service occupations as specialists in terrorism reporting.

The hopes for individual states to establish an augmentation program to assist in law enforcement, antiterrorism officers, and more specialized but simple training for emergency responders in antiterrorism assessments could prevent or mitigate future terrorism actions. Future safety is in jeopardy with the current practices of antiterrorism. The United States federal agencies and individual state police departments are running thin with the demands of protection in terms of terrorism today. Terrorists have time to plan whereas all public safety providers react daily to a plethora of domestic problems.

There is potential for error from public service providers when cyber technology continues to be such an integral part of daily lives in America. Cyber-crimes and cyberspace are not just concerns of the future. All aspects of life are controlled by technology that accesses capability beyond human reach. Technology has made occupations more adaptable. The same technology has also made it more accessible for hackers and terrorists to research and tamper with critical infrastructure to cause harm, such as shutting down an electrical grid, shifting rail routes, and confusing maritime-container car placements. This is a serious long-term security concern. The media has a profound role in producing information, and it needs special attention to antiterrorism so it can aid in reporting antiterrorism procedures that individual state departments of homeland security establish. Media increasingly impacts people in America, and the manner the media broadcasts information can shape the public's emotional response to terrorism.

The United States infrastructure will continue to be a top concern for protection. Antiterrorism has evolved over the years as we as a nation have learned from terrorist attacks. The history of terrorism has placed fear in society, but the United States must be proactive on such a threat rather than reactive as demonstrated during September 11, 2001 terrorist attacks. Using antiterrorism tools will assist in making decisions toward mitigation, security measures, and deterrence. For the United States to be more proactive on antiterrorism matters it must depend on the enforcement of the developed antiterrorism methodology. Antiterrorism is an integrated risk-management system that demands a working relationship of all public safety officials from federal to local levels, thus allowing for more and shared resources. Terrorism may not be eliminated, but the massive responsibility in antiterrorism efforts will aid in physical security, operational response and recovery, shared intelligence between agencies at all levels, information gathering that counters terrorism, and security programs for private corporations and businesses to at least have levels of deterrence. The threat of terrorism is real, but as Americans work together we can prevent terrorist attack.

Chapter 12

WHAT IS BASIC TERRORISM PREVENTION?

SINCE THE TERRORIST attacks on American soil took place on September 11, 2001 the focus and energy of the United States government toward counterterrorism measures has been focused on policies and strategies. One strategy developed was the creation of the Department of Homeland Security, Transportation Security Administration (TSA). TSA is a valued asset in airports and carries much responsibility. The personnel uniform resemble law-enforcement uniforms, but limited training among other things prevents them from acting as law-enforcement officials for the United States. If the United States government invests heavily in deterrence as a counterterrorism strategy, TSA would best serve as official, uniformed, law-enforcement personnel. If this became true, then TSA could participate in a leading terrorism prevention tool that all uniformed law-enforcement agencies conduct, which is the execution of a basic traffic stop or pedestrian stop. Traffic stops conducted by law-enforcement officers nationwide identify localized crime to extremism.

One independent situation worth mentioning is a traffic stop conducted by a state trooper in Oklahoma. Timothy McVeigh was stopped in 1995 by a state police officer after the bombing for not having a license plate on the vehicle (Cid 2009). The trooper did not know that the driver of the vehicle was a domestic terrorist. If the trooper had other obligations to the community, McVeigh may have gotten away with the bombing. This did not prevent the attack from happening, but extra uniformed officers can easily deter acts of terror, and Transportation Security Agency already has a good uniformed presence that supports deterrence.

Traffic stops conducted by law enforcement officers can prevent terrorism. This proactive law-enforcement tool uncovered intentional terrorism in Richmond, Virginia (IACP, n.a.). A police officer noticed a dark van parked with its lights off, which was suspicious for the area, so the officer approached the vehicle and was informed by the occupants that they were lost. The officer gave directions to the two men in the van, but the officers investigation later discovered that they were plotting an attack in Richmond with the assistance of a third man (McCorm 2009).

Community contact is more common with a patrol officer; the same applies to TSA when conducting their duties in airports. There is chance that there are members of terrorist organizations within the communities officers are patrolling and among the people TSA agents are screening at airports (Alexander and Moras 2004). Police officers will only make contact with imbedded terrorists through means of traffic stops or subject contact (Alexander and Moras 2004). Subject contact is a pedestrian stop or a Terry stop conducted by police officers of a person or people due to suspicious or illegal activity identified by police or citizens. Motor vehicle, rail, and air travel are the means by which people survive in the United States economic system; it will be no surprise that terrorists use motor vehicles, subways, or airlines to obtain jobs, rent homes or apartments, and buy products in furtherance of their terrorist activities (Alexander and Moras 2004).

Knowing that modes of transportation feed and fuel opportunity for both terrorists and everyday people, traffic stops and pedestrian stops force intervention that could potentially prevent catastrophes of tremendous proportions. Here are addition examples of the importance of traffic stops conducted by law-enforcement officers worldwide:

(1) Swiss police conducted a traffic stop on three eco-terrorists in the mist of conducting an attack against the IBM Corporate Headquarters near Zurich (Johnson 2010).

(2) Police officers in North Sumatra, province of Indonesia, arrested six terrorists after conducting a traffic stop on a suspicious van (Yursal and Arnaz 2010). There were eight individuals in the van; two escaped capture from police.

(3) Four of the hijackers that conducted the attacks on September 11, 2001 were stopped and given citations by police for vehicle code violations (USA Today 2008). Al-Hazmi received a speeding ticket in Oklahoma that he paid by mail. Mohamed Atta was stopped for speeding in Florida. Hani Hani Hanjour was stopped for speeding in Arlington, Virginia, and Ziad Jarrah was also stopped for speeding in Maryland (USA Today 2008). This did not prevent the attack, but proves the potential of contact made with terrorists by law enforcement officers at all levels while conducting traffic stops for motor vehicle violations.

(4) A Goose Creek County South Carolina Deputy Sheriff discovered bomb-making material in a vehicle after conducting a traffic stop for speeding (Burton and Stewart, n.a). This traffic stop revealed that the two Middle Eastern men were planning to make explosives.

Transportation and money also feed the United States infrastructure and TSA plays a large role in infrastructure protection. This role was identified when the Aviation and Transportation Security Act established the Transportation Security Administration (TSA) to protect the transportation system and ensure the freedom of movement for people and commerce' (DHS website 2012). TSA can easily require an annual budget of $8.1 billion dollars and 58,000 personnel. TSA's mission is to "maximize transportation protection and security in response to the evolving terrorist threat while protecting passengers" privacy and facilitating the flow of legal commerce" (DHS 2012). The responsibility that TSA has for the transportation system involves plenty of vulnerabilities in the areas of aviation, rail, mass transit, highway, pipeline, and ports (DHS website 2012). These systems are "designed to move people and commerce quickly to their destinations" (DHS 2012) throughout the nation. It is difficult for TSA to provide effective security strategies in these vulnerable environments without the authority and jurisdiction of law-enforcement officials, especially "while maintaining quick and easy access for passengers and cargo" (DHS 2012).

According to the Department of Homeland Security website under TSA, the mission of TSA is not the only responsibility each agent has in protecting America's infrastructure, it also includes:

(1) Ensuring effective and efficient screening of all aviation passengers, baggage, and air cargo on passenger planes.

(2) Deploying Federal Air Marshal plain clothes law-enforcement officials, internationally and domestically to detect, deter, and defeat hostile acts targeting air carriers, airports, passengers, and crews.

(3) Managing security risks of the surface transportation systems by working with federal, local, and private stakeholders, providing support and programmatic direction, and conducting onsite inspections.

(4) Developing and implementing more efficient, reliable, integrated, and cost-effective screening programs.

(5) Working with stakeholders to manage the security risk to the US surface transportation system while ensuring freedom of movement of people and commerce (DHS website 2012).

These responsibilities, without law enforcement authority, cover "approximately 625 million domestic and international aviation passengers per year; 751 million passengers traveling on buses each year; more than 9 billion passenger trips on mass transit per year; nearly 800,000 shipments of hazardous materials transported every day (95 percent by truck); more than 140,000 miles of railroad track (of which 120,000 miles are privately owned); 3.8 million miles of roads (46,717 miles of Interstate highway and 114,700 miles of National Highway System roads); 582,000 bridges over 20 feet of span; 54 tunnels over 19,685 feet in length; and nearly 2.5 million miles of pipeline" (DHS website 2012). The TSA depends on the $8.1 billion dollar annual budget to implement effective transportation security measures. In addition, "public confidence in the safety and security of the Nation's transportation systems ensures the continued success and growth of the transportation industry" (DHS website 2012).

In order to ensure quality protection the Department of Homeland Security and TSA conducts an annual Surface Transportation Security Priority Assessment (DHS website 2012). This assessment tool develops relationships through engagement with federal, state, local, and tribal government partners. DHS and TSA wanted to ensure there was a comprehensive framework of recommendations to enhance surface transportation security. "The Assessment reflects President Obama's commitment to coordinating surface transportation security efforts among all government partners and the private sector to enhance security; reduce risk; improve the efficiency and effectiveness of federal security capabilities; strengthen interactive stakeholder partnerships; and streamline security management coordination to protect Americans from threats of terrorism" (DHS website 2012). TSA can easily fulfill this obligation with law-enforcement authority and training and not rely entirely on state, county, and local law enforcement agencies to conduct prevention operations. It can be a shared responsibility between government and local law enforcement.

There are many changing factors when conducting terrorism prevention. Even with all the military and law-enforcement efforts toward such matters, there will always be the chances of attacks conducted by extreme terrorist organizations. One consideration regarding terrorism prevention is the economy. Funding granted by the United States to the highway systems is dependent on taxes levied on the nation's gas and oil. Twenty-three percent of the tax is given to the Department of Transportation (104th Congress 1995). The highway systems are the direct responsibility of state governments to repair, construct, and address safety conditions (104th Congress 1995). If the federal government places most responsibility on state governments, there is potential for repairs, construction, and safety conditions to be missed.

In 1995, states presented recommendations to the Department of Transportation (DOT) to improve the national highway system; this later became the National Highway System Designation Act of 1995. The recommendation presented were repairs of roadways and laws of federal aviation (104th Congress 1995). The recommendations from states placed the DOT as a shareholder of the highway systems since the United States government would allocate a percentage of the DOT annual budget approvals toward all fifty states and US territories under the guidance of chapter 1 of title 23 of the United States Code (104th Congress 1995). Money from DOT is now also granted to the most critical infrastructure based on population and obligation as directed in the Intermodal Surface Transportation Efficiency Act of 1991, which led to a clearer definition of highway systems under federal aid (104th Congress 1995). According to the National Highway System Designation Act of 1995,

> The National Highway System consists of the highway routes and connections to transportation facilities depicted on the map submitted by the Secretary to Congress with the report entitled "Pulling Together: The National Highway System and its Connections to Major Intermodal Terminals" and dated May 24, 1996. The system serves major population centers, international border crossings, ports, airports, public transportation facilities, and other intermodal transportation facilities, and other major travel destinations that meet national defense requirements, and serve interstate and interregional travel (104th Congress page 1-68 1995).

The raw number of total budget authority allocated to the Department of Homeland Security in 2012 was $56,983,449,000 (DHS 2012). TSA consumed 14 percent, but will receive 13 percent in 2013. In 2012, TSA was granted $105.2 million dollars and 535 position openings that accommodated the purchase, installation, and operation of Advanced Imaging Technology (AIT) at airport checkpoints (DHS 2012). In addition to the AITs, there was also the development of Explosive Detection Systems, Explosive Trace Detection units, Advanced X-Ray systems, and Bottled Liquid Scanners (DHS 2012). These assets were part of the American Recovery and Reinvestment Act (ARRA Public Law 111-5). In part of the 14 percent spent, TSA developed a behavior recognition and response training program (DHS 2012). They incorporated it into the voluntary crewmember self-defense program (DHS 2012). Both training programs are examples of TSA responsibility and layer of security they provide. Another layered security defense that TSA uses their budget for goes toward the cargo screening (DHS 2012). Prior to 9/11 there were no multiple-layered security procedures for air cargo (DHS 2012). TSA now has procedures for known and established shippers to ship cargo on domestic passenger flights (DHS 2012). This responsibility was enacted in 2010 under the 9/11 Commission Act (P.L. 110-53). This Act also allowed Customs and Border Patrol and TSA to work side-by-side in a joint technology pilot project that enhanced the sharing of electronic shipping information (DHS 2012). This improved the identification process of high-risk cargo.

The budget plan for 2012 maintained the Federal Air Marshal Service. Its responsibilities are immediate response to terrorism aboard flights both internationally and domestically (DHS 2012). The FAMS is the primary-law enforcement entity within TSA (DHS 2012). Twelve-point four million dollars was dedicated to expanding the watch-list initiative so TSA is enabled to identify individuals who may present a threat to passenger air travel (DHS 2012). One-hundred-twenty-five point seven million dollars sustained the TSA's 900 canine teams used at checkpoint screening at airports, to assist in cargo screening, and to enhance security in the mass transit environment (DHS 2012). Aviation security has increased in cost by 400 percent (DHS 2012). Each year becomes more costly, and each budget proposal makes progress toward fulfilling the intent of the Aviation and Transportation Security Act. The 1 percent granted to science and technology of the 2012 and 2013 budget can be more beneficial toward federal law-enforcement training for TSA credentials. Science and technology can apply for grants to make up the difference lost. TSA carries the primary role of screening 100 percent of passengers from flights within or bound for the United States (DHS 2012). The screening helps prevent misidentification of passengers who have names similar to watch-list names that the United States government developed from information sharing with intelligence service domestically and internationally.

The secretary of Homeland Security should add TSA to Title 40 of the USC under paragraph 1315 as law-enforcement authority. Since TSA has so much responsibility to the public and it resembles a law-enforcement uniformed presence, this addition will allow TSA officers and agents to "protect the buildings, grounds, and property that is owned, occupied, or secured by federal government" (Cornell Law website 2012); this authority granted by the secretary of Homeland Security is supported by the Homeland Security Act of 2002. This opportunity would free up current local law-enforcement officers protecting perimeters of airports to conduct routine patrol duties that could lead to more traffic stops being conducted in hopes of catching terrorism in the making. Other considerations for TSA to capitalize on with law enforcement authority under Title 40 is the enforcement of laws extended outside federal property under memorandums of agreement between the secretary of Homeland Security and local law-enforcement agencies. According to the Cornell University College of Law's website, "For the protection of property owned or occupied by the federal government and persons on the property, the Secretary may enter into agreements with federal agencies and with state and local governments to obtain authority for officers and agents designated under this section to enforce federal laws and state and local laws concurrently with other federal law enforcement officers and with state and local law enforcement officers" (Cornell Law website 2012). This would provide opportunity for TSA officers and agents to conduct traffic stops when traveling in official status to and from government facilities, marine ports, and airports, and more.

TSA is responsible for enhancing security at major local transportation facilities. This program is called Visible Intermodal Prevention and Response (VIPR) (TSA 2007). The establishment of this program was due to the Madrid train bombings. TSA took initiative and placed more emphasis on enhancing security on rail and mass-transit systems nationwide. The program is broken into teams, and the teams "Comprised of federal air marshals, surface transportation security inspectors, transportation security officers, behavior detection officers and explosives detection canine teams, VIPR teams over the past two years have augmented security at key transportation facilities in urban areas around the country, including New York City, Buffalo and Syracuse, N.Y., Los Angeles, Boston and Providence, R.I." (TSA website 2007).

These teams require local law-enforcement support to provide security resources, a deterrent presence, and detect capabilities to disrupt potential terrorist planning activities. Instead of taking local law-enforcement off the streets of their community to supply assistance to VIPR, TSA uniformed personnel could assume the responsibility. The VIPR program is doing well. It is reaching all volumes of transportation systems nationwide while "Working closely with our transportation partners and law enforcement, which ensures resources are deployed efficiently and in a complementary fashion, providing an effective first line of defense against terrorism" (TSA website 2007). "Where is a terrorist more apt to be found? Not on an airplane these days—more likely on the interstate," says Tennessee Department of Safety & Homeland Security Commissioner Bill Gibbons (Gomez 2011).

Not only does TSA conduct VIPR operations, but TSA is also working with local law-enforcement agencies nationwide under a program called Highway Watch. This program allows local law-enforcement agencies to work with highway and delivery personnel. The highway and delivery personnel are important assets to law enforcement since millions of miles of highways, vast numbers of bridges, tunnels, and overpasses are driven or repaired by the transportation system personnel (Davies and Plotkin 2005). The Highway Watch program ensures that TSA and local law-enforcement is collecting information pertaining to infrastructure security from commercial truck drivers, commercial bus drivers, school-bus drivers, maintenance crews, and bridge and tunnel toll collectors (Davies and Plotkin 2005). These in-the-field operations conducted by TSA also lead to their connection to the United States Coast Guard. TSA has a role in the Sensitive Security Information designation. They share this responsibility with the United States Coast Guard (Chertoff 2009). It shows how much responsibility TSA has, but not the authority and training it needs. Changes need to be considered to accommodate future terrorism deterrence planning.

It is important to have a deterrence plan toward terrorism using empirical data rather than simply personal experience, to create assumptions of future attacks (Cid 2008). The attacks on the World Trade Center's created an opinion that more attacks will be against greater symbols, just as the attack of the federal building in Oklahoma created opinions that radical groups would target more federal buildings (Cid 2008). Neither came true as terrorism is evolving in tactics, financial wealth, recruitment, and social blending. Placing TSA in a law-enforcement role will incorporate it into the counterterrorism realms with more conventional policing (Cid 2008). There are currently approximately 750,000 uniformed officers in the United States who possess counterterrorism skills due to the nation's community policing requirements (Cid 2008); adding uniformed TSA Agents will only increase the number of uniformed presence. According to Cid, "In order to commit an act of terrorism, terrorist must engage in certain preparatory actions such as acquisition of materials, and target surveillance" (Cid 2008, 7). Through behavior indicators, uniformed law-enforcement officers can identify these actions and identify minor infractions of law that place all uniformed law-enforcement officers into a position to execute pedestrian stops or traffic stops, which could potentially lead to arresting terrorists.

Having more uniformed police officers is a force multiplier in terrorism prevention; moreover, it also provides more players in crime prevention, which equals more protection. The protection of mankind within the United States is also tempered by weapon law interpretation. A society protected by guns is respected and not threatened to change its character from the influence of other nations. In addition, people feel safe when they know protection is a priority, such as the Second Amendment. The Second Amendment is a crime and terrorism prevention tool.

Every good criminal can be recruited as a terrorist, but every terrorist needs the skills of a criminal to make money for their cause.

Chapter 13

WHO IS DOING IT RIGHT?

MANY AGENCIES IN the emergency services are doing well in emergency response to terrorism, but no agency are heard more on the news than the Department of Homeland Security and New York City Police Department. I decided to find reports they published, one from each agency. Both reports can be located online (web access) for public viewing. With this mentioned, I want to share two reports that both agencies produced since it ties into chapter one. There is much value to these reports. In efforts to explain both reports I conducted a comparative analysis of the Department of Homeland Security Right-wing Extremism Report and the New York City Police Department Radicalization Report is to ensure a non-biased approach toward both reports, both are public reports found on the Internet.

On April 7, 2009, the Department of Homeland Security published an unclassified report from the Office of Intelligence and Analysis regarding right-wing extremism that was distributed to counterterrorism and law enforcement officials within the United States. This report is only one of many reports conducted by Homeland Security about right-wing terrorism. The primary purpose of the report is to provide information to counterterrorism and law-enforcement officials so they can deter, prevent, and plan for the response to terrorist attacks. Between 2009 and 2011, the New York City Police

Department's Intelligence Division published a report on their official website concerning homegrown threats in the city of New York. The Intelligence Division conducted research on homegrown terrorism that captured trends internationally and within the United States.

The research question that the Department of Homeland Security Intelligence and Analysis Assessment reported was the phenomenon of violent radicalization in the United States (Department of Homeland Security 2009). After reading the report, it seems to lack in research. The primary source of information came from the Federal Bureau of Investigation. This seems sufficient for what the report intended. The Federal Bureau of Investigation is the lead law-enforcement agency for all terrorism incidents or any activity considered to lead to possible terrorism (Kamien 2006, 1056). After the September 11, 2001 attacks conducted by terrorist using aircraft, the Federal Bureau of Investigation looked into hundreds of thousands of tips that could relate to terrorism (Kamien 2006, 1057). With this understanding, the literature that Department of Homeland Security utilized to publish an extremism report came from all research that was collected by the Federal Bureau of Investigation since 2001 from all investigations they were involved with. This topic of importance shouldn't be established on only one source. This report did not have any sophisticated research method applied that collaborated the purpose of the assessments. The report could have benefited from scientific research that supports a theory and hypothesis. Since the report is structured for providing information to colleagues in law enforcement, it is qualitative. The Federal Bureau of Investigation used the informant process of research to collect their data from defined cases experienced in the Bureau and law enforcement agencies throughout the United States. All data collected by the Federal Bureau of Investigation from law-enforcement agencies throughout the United States regarding right-wing extremism supports the emphasis and conclusion the report intended to achieve (Department of Homeland Security 2009).

New York City Police Department's Intelligence Division geared their report on domestic terrorism toward policy makers and law-enforcement officials throughout the United States (Silber and Bhatt

2012). There were four pages of sources that supported the research conducted by the New York City Police Department's Intelligence Division. The literature supported the current terrorism threat in America, the radicalization process, New York City experience of terrorism during September 11, 2001 attacks to date the report was published, and implications of domestic terrorism (Silber and Bhatt 2012). The research design included collecting, analyzing, and interpreting sources, which supported their hypothesis of domestic terrorism concerns, which is explanatory research. The Intelligence Division's method in research is both quantitative and qualitative. Seeking sources that provide the history and process of radicalization and the economic effect of terrorism incidents used the quantitative method. The next method used was qualitative, which was contributed from the experience that New York City has lived from domestic terrorism events, proving that New York City is considered a likely target to include five other locations in the United States and five other locations internationally (Silber and Bhatt 2012). This data was collected from news articles and media producers and officials from the ten locations where terrorism is likely to occur indicated by past or recent incidents. The presented data in the Intelligence Division's report was supported by the sources researched and supported the conclusion about domestic terrorism.

Both reports provide the appropriate level of analysis toward the audience presented. The Department of Homeland Security was only addressing law enforcement officials, so sourcing only the Federal Bureau of Investigation is enough validation since all local law enforcement and federal agencies conduct information sharing (Kamien 2009, 361). The report conducted by the New York City Police Department was overwhelmingly detailed because of the report's audience. Policy makers need abundant and accurate information to support future laws or legislation that protects the American people. New York City Police conducted their analysis thoroughly compared to Department of Homeland Security, but the research methodology gathered for both reports was appropriate considering the purpose of each report. Both reports have weaknesses: they reported trends of cultures and incidents that change. This type of fluctuating reporting needs to be readdressed occasionally to identify old trends or advise on new trends that place America at risk of a domestic terrorism incident, which will make both reports more effective, but both reports educate the public. If educating the public is a must on the matters, the reporting needs to veer from culture profiling. The world is currently more sensitive on profiling than safety from terrorism.

A paper resume may prove great ability from your past, but wisdom of those that surround you will guide you to greatness.

Chapter 14

HAS RACISM BECOME AN ISSUE DUE TO TERRORISM?

ONE WOULD HOPE that racism is no longer an issue in our modern world of many diverse cultures, yet it certainly plays a role in terrorism. Racism is a complex topic. Racism stems from the idea that one race is inherently superior to another race. Racism or prejudice and hostility against Jews are called anti-Semitism. Some acts of terrorism are rooted in anti-Semitism, yet at the same time Arabs in today's society are receiving similar treatment because of terrorism.

During the Great Depression of the 1930s in the United States, racism against blacks was fueled by competition between whites and blacks for jobs. In the 1960s, racial profiling of black people led to violence against them. While race relations have improved since the Civil Rights Movement, racism still exists in today's American society. The negative racial profiling creates resentment and mistrust among all people, especially in a minority community. If America is the land of the free, why is there still a stigma of racism or institutionalized racism? Reading Harper Lee's *To Kill a Mockingbird*, could lead you to believe that the United States institutionalized racism. The United States of America represents the land of diversity and multiculturalism, yet in reality not all people are respected.

Racism and Anti-Semitism will continue to be a concern due to ignorance and the freedom people have to sponsor groups that advertize such hatred. This is unbelievable, especially when the United States established Constitutional Amendments after the Civil War and the New Deal after the Depression. The Amendments were established for equal protection, mainly the Fourteenth Amendment. The New Deal had to be enacted twice, because the first policy did not include the support of the very poor and the majority of the working (blue collar) class.

Life in America happens in full circle and even in 2012 events motivated by racism still occurred. According to US Newswire, "A growing list of domestic extremists is seeking to enflame the situation surrounding the shooting death of Trayvon Martin by George Zimmerman in Sanford, Florida (ADL, 2013). According to the Anti-Defamation League (ADL), various white supremacists and black racist groups are exploiting publicity surrounding the case and promoting racism, hatred and even anti-Semitism" (Gutnick online article 2012). Freedom granted by the Constitution of the United States allows for diversity and opportunity. There is no person greater than another in the pursuit of happiness and freedom. Respect for others regardless of differences is a matter of humanity and human rights.

While it would be too easy to dismiss every freedom of speech demonstration that presents racism or anti-Semitism, in fact, individual states offer laws that prohibited profane and negative content in accordance to the Constitution of the United States. The First Amendment offers freedom of assembly, meaning that people of the United States of America have the individual right to come together and express in a collective fashion what is wrong politically or to attempt to preserve human rights. These assemblies must be peaceful. According to Dwight D. Eisenhower, "A nation's hope of lasting peace cannot be firmly based upon any race in armaments but rather upon just relations and honest understanding with all other nations" (Dwight D. Eisenhower, 1953 speech). This speech regarded the respect of multiculturalism throughout the world. Unfortunately, while Americans heard this speech, many did not was heard but not listen. Mississippi did recognize the reality of racism and racial violence and eventually established laws against violence towards black people.

According to a speech President Obama gave in 2008, "America can only transcend the cruel legacies of race and racism when blacks no longer bear the burden of speaking out on race and racism, when whites bear their own historic racial crosses." The fact that he was forced to repudiate and explain his former pastor, revealed a complex social gospel. America has a long way to go to build a more multiracial, (The Zeleza Post 2008).

RACISM AND EDUCATION

Proper education starting at an early age regarding racism or anti-Semitism can lead a child away from forming a distorted perception of reality. Mildred D. Taylor's children's book, *Roll of Thunder, Hear My Cry*, describes a black family sharecropping in the field with white people, but the blacks were subject to mistreatment while the white people were not. Despite our country's attempt to lay multicultural foundations for our younger generations, racism and violence associated with racism as displayed in *Roll of Thunder, Hear My Cry* still occur.

According to Roger Phillips, "Roseline Seporgan's second-grade class was learning about heroes. Dr. King was the launching point. Brandy DeAlba's eighth-grade English class watched a movie about 9/11, which would lead to lessons on racism, anti-Semitism and a reading of Anne Frank's diary. If every school had teachers unafraid to educate the youth of America about the harsh reality the United States has evolved from, diversity in the country would be more acceptable. Multicultural diversity is displayed in communities nationwide, and as children grow they carry forward the attitudes and behaviors they observe from adults. It is difficult to prevent childrens' total exposure to racism and anti-Semitism.

Discrimination is still a problem in the United States, and treatment of children while in a school setting should be considered. Schools are a collected synergy of religious believers and ethnicities. After the September 11, 2001 terrorist attacks, Arab American children were profiled since the terrorists that conducted the attacks had a Muslim connection (Daraisch 2012). The American public once again showed discrimination due to a significant event. An article written by Isra Daraisch suggests that civil rights for humanity are not a focus in the American education system; she continued to elaborate on what civil rights are by including a passage from The Civil Right Act of 1964 reading:

> Racial or ethnic harassment is unlawful. It can deny or limit a student's ability to receive or participate in the benefits, services, or opportunities in a school's program - simply speaking it denies students the right to an education free of discrimination. The existence of a racially hostile environment that is encouraged, accepted, or tolerated by a school, college, or university constitutes different treatment of students on the basis of race (Daraisch 2012, 5).

Providing education at a young age regarding the Constitution and racism and anti-Semitism could lead to a broader understanding of race as an observable fact in life. According to Julius Lester,

> Racism is an exceedingly complex, tricky, and confusing phenomenon. This is so because racism is often indiscriminately extended and applied to non-biological and nonracial groupings - nations, linguistic groups, ethnic or cultural groups. For example, Jews are not a race and anti-Semitism was not expressed in the language of racism until the 19th century, but the religious and political expressions of anti-Semitism that roll through Western Civilization like a mighty and polluted river are racist (Lester 2000).

Furthermore, this level of intercultural learning in the education system will allow the younger generation of the United States to reflect on moral values and assumptions. This can only take place if well-trained teachers have more sensitive methods to ensure individual diversity in every class from now into later generations.

Racism and anti-Semitism impede healthy dialogue on race and impose morally on society. Not only do they affect the education system, they also impact employment and access to goods and services. It is important to understand the morality of society. The United States surrounds itself with moral issues that present happiness or deepen sorrow through suffering. Truth be told, racism and violent racial acts are a human rights matter. The issue surrounding racism fails to provide equal living rights and full participation in society to all individuals suffering from racism. Human rights are developed to entitle people the opportunity to be free from suffering as a result of choices politicians or everyday citizens make. "We the People" need to unite as one to share the freedoms that many of our countrymen and women gallantly gave their lives for.

Discrimination and racism against individual people who are Arab, Muslim, Jewish, Indian/Native American, African American, Mexican American, and other ethnicities and religions create a terrible perception about people in society. This social evil will continue until individual differences are accepted in all geographic locations of America. It would take years through childhood upbringing and education for people to develop logical outcomes to their beliefs. The land of the free has experienced numerous events through history that prevents the lifting of hatred toward individuals, but teaching the leaders of tomorrow can benefit society with the knowledge of Constitutional Rights and Moral obligation to all people.

Racial profiling in the war on terrorism: warfare philosophy is dependent on trust, cooperation, and respect between states when engaged in war. A practice of racial profiling will create resentment and mistrust between military services and identity of host nations people as conflict worsens or absorbed negatively by viewers. In all respects, racial profiling is racism. Racism will always lead to anger of the profiled group and ultimately build walls between communications. This may prevents diplomacy and humanitarian requirements.

Let's review history: Affirmative action was established to aid in equal employment and education due to previous lack of civil rights, even after the Civil Rights Act was enacted. Both represent the end of discrimination. Laws are paper without enforcement, and laws granted are not always right for the people. Affirmative action and the Civil Rights Act proved we are not reading and following the Constitution as written to protect our union as Americans, specifically the Fourteenth Amendment. This is an area that places our country in a diverse direction. Diversity means division, when all Americans should have common ground and language. The character of America is one color and speaks one common language, which is freedom.

The American culture has a philosophy dependent upon trust, cooperation, and respect between all people regardless of race.

Chapter 15

IS IT JUSTIFIED?

We can't blame religion for the horrific actions taken against
innocent people; it is the choices that extreme believers use to
initiate harm against others.

TERRORISM HAS CREATED resentment, and mistrust. Terrorism is still
taking place with spontaneous attacks and killings, which prove
that the conflict is worsening. What makes this emotion worse is the
propaganda or considerations that all terrorism is linked to the Islam
community. This is racial profiling. Racial profiling is racism. Racism
will always lead to anger of profiled group and ultimately build walls
between communications. This prevents diplomacy and humanitarian
requirements. Truth be told, terrorism has been used for thousands of
years, but more noticeable as beliefs shared by terrorists and tactics
become more advanced.

The actions taken by any person who kills innocent people
are morally wrong, but there is strong foundation for such action
conducted due to the external causes that effect terrorist ideology.
People can be provoked beyond emotional control. Politics and
military action can provoke people to hate; in turn, this hatred leads
to attacks conducted by terrorism groups. This determinism provides
no free will in humans that participate in terrorism attacks. Terrorists

believe that they shouldn't be held morally and legally responsible since they are conducting these actions under the aegis of a higher power, Allah. Allah cannot justify such evil against all people who do not believe in Islam, and those who conduct such crimes should be punished regardless of the ideology that initiated the terrorism operation. People that participate in this activity are ethically, morally, and psychologically wrongly programmed for all societies that wish to live without fear. There is fear in the United States and throughout the world due to terrorism. Many people believe that religion influenced such behavior.

Planned terrorist attacks conducted throughout the world by Islamic extremist caused fear throughout the world. As Leslie Miller, stated, "The United States government was confronted with a serious problem that surrounded the searching of passengers of airliners . . ." not necessarily Muslim (Miller 2004, 12). For example, Homeland Security was searching people for explosives because of a Chechen woman, who in 2004 carried explosives onto two different airliners where they later detonated (Miller 2004). This action proved the fear of the world. Terrorism could be planned and executed by any person. For example, in 1993, a non-Muslim American attacked the World Trade Center (Kamien 2006). On the other hand, non-Muslim Americans also executed the attacks on the Oklahoma Federal Building and the Atlanta Olympics, yet it is Arabs and Muslims usually portrayed as fanatical, violence-loving maniacs (Clegg 2003). As a result, decision makers sometimes operate on the basis of an ingrained assumption that Arabs and Muslims are terrorists (Clegg 2003), but the recent shooting at a movie theater in Colorado was an ill, emotional, American native.

Terrorism is all over the world and being conducted by random groups with ideologies. Since the Greek and Roman era, philosophers such as Cicero have elaborated on theoretic justification for going to war and conduct of soldiers/warriors fighting during war. Historians have written about such things in military strategy books of today's operations. Cicero's theory of "just war" has assisted current governments in the reasoning for taking human life, as taking life is wrong, but essential for states to protect their citizens with the intentions of promoting justice. Islam extremists and terrorists can view the just war theory as justified support to fulfill their ideology against western civilization per the Declaration of War against Western Civilization by Osama Bin Laden, but understanding of Sharia law may provide facts to Muslim faith.

In my opinion, there are two approaches to this matter. That is deontological theory or teleological theory. Both theories mention the relationship between good versus evil. This topic is vague and perceives different theories of good versus bad choices even if actions of an individual's occupation are determinism justified. Deontological theory is moral or not, good intentions or act can influence outcomes, regardless if the matter turned consequential or favorable. I feel that this is more toward an individual who is attempting to make a mark in life and fails to look out for others. Possible action could bring negative balance that doesn't benefit either good or evil. Men and women follow orders and trust their government that the right choice has already been made. Individual people in situations should understand if an act is right or wrong without committing to such actions, terrorist rarely think what is right or wrong prior to an attack. I feel that this can be considered common sense, or an individual who is caring enough to think the matter through completely, but too sensitive to react. There is a simple rule of thumb in figuring right from wrong: think of human rights when justifying determination of action as each matter is different. Using this rule of thumb in determinations allow more understanding in human behavior of moral value through good and bad decision. This thought process pertains to all people and groups of people, since the personality of each person is faltered by surroundings or cultures. Pain, pleasure, knowledge, freedom, and physical objects, which we are all familiar with, are a non-moral process. I call this "Creatures Comforts of Life." A definitive standard of wrong or right is a non-moral outcome that is believed to be more beneficial toward good over evil, but what is good, and what is evil? The reasonable person would believe good as being policies or laws created to meet the daily life and safety of all people. An act is only good and should only be done if the rule leans more toward good than evil, which terrorist can easily play off of. Moral value is dependent on the non-moral value brought about. The two theories discussed clearly mentioned moral obligations to an ideology or protection of the greater good, which many lean on religion to answer the right from wrong. Both of them combined can be the approach of a utilitarian.

Analyzing utilitarianism and its focus on rule over action, and briefly analyzing rule utilitarianism and its focus on rule over action like the Golden Rule "Do unto others as you would have them do unto you," making an argument for how this can be both ethical and unethical. Rule Utilitarianism is defined as "emphasizes the centrality of rules in morality and insists that we are generally, if not always, to tell what to do in particular situations by appeal to a rule like that of truth-telling rather than by asking what particular action will have the best consequences in the situation in question." (Frankena online article 1973). This means that we are looking to care or make life easier for the better good, really similar to aforementioned. Now we can lead into the Golden Rule. People should be willing to do right for others without expecting anything in return. At the same time, if a murder takes place, committing another murder doesn't make it right. It is concerning when the world we face will become engulfed in greed as recessions grown and world infrastructure continues to falter to the needs of people.

Most people throughout the world view terrorism as violent acts against innocent people in domestic society (Christopher 2004). How is such evil related to religion? International society has deemed terrorism acts of any nature as "to harm others in a surprising manner by use of bombs being detonated, murder or mutilation of those of different religions or tribes, and use of public transportation of any kind as a weapon to kill innocent people" (Christopher 2004, 186). There are hundreds of other acts of terrorism as defined by other state and non-state governments that make it extremely hard to accurately establish a true definition of terrorism. This doesn't make terrorism a biased term by governments in power to delegitimize those with little power since most cultures disagree with the use of violence against innocent people of society. What is hard to accept is that people "who perform terrorism acts deeply believe they are just, as they proclaim themselves as freedom fighters or warriors of justice," not as terrorists (Christopher 2004). The twist in terms is the nature of bias beliefs being made to support any group or party with aim to achieve terrorism goals.

Moreover, freedom fighters do not consider themselves terrorists but believe that they are ridding the world of evil by raging war against any state or group that disagrees with their beliefs or threatens their culture (Smilansky 2010). How is that freedom? Terrorists use violent acts against any person or persons belonging to any state or group that supports political agendas that differ from the morality of terrorism. It is difficult to place terrorism in a category of war, but it can be considered non-confrontational war. Terrorist groups are not officially states or even non-states. Indirectly, terrorism and the acts or tactics used by freedom fighters can be war of other means through the justification of their beliefs and a known enemy. In reality, the Roman Empire was the most powerful in its day but lost that superior standing due to politics and economy ravished by acts of terrorism. The Roman Empire then is America today as it struggles to maintain military and diplomatic strengths due to the $15,863,489,715,103 of debt (US Debt Clock 2012).

The concept that Cicero had regarding warfare was treated as a last result when questioned nations never responded to the diplomacy. That is the same with the United States and evident by the 187 embassies, consulates, and legations throughout the world that represent the United States of America when addressing the Iraqi and Afghanistan conflicts prior to military involvement. Similar to Cicero, America truly defends their allies, which aids in resolving global issues. As for "*jus ad bellum*," America has checks and balances through diplomacy before declaring war. Diplomatic missions through the Department of State offer opportunity to make peaceful settlements prior to the initiation of hostilities (Christopher 2004). It is unsure if this form of diplomacy is perfect. I can only imagine the daunting pressure placed on individuals required to make decisions toward human rights concerns. According to the Declaration of

War Proclamation written by Osama Bin Laden, "America is evil" (Declaration of War Against Western Civilization online article 2010). America may be evil regarding the ideology he stemmed from, but America doesn't have organizations that seek a particular society and establish planning that causes mass killings or casualties from generated attacks against that culture.

The justification of war can be argued when terrorism acts are spontaneous, but follow similar Just War tenets as states do when executed under their beliefs. Terrorists feel that western civilization is a civilization of evildoers (Smilansky 2010). Augustine stated, "War may not be undertaken without rightful intentions, such as the advancement of good, the securing of peace, the punishment of evildoers, or the avoidance of evil" (Christopher 2004, 51). This proves Just Cause for terrorist organizations to commit acts of violence under their beliefs and Augustine's theory of Just War since terrorists believe they need to punish evildoers. Terrorist organizations' higher authority is Allah, according to the Declaration of War Against Western Civilization, and this is their proper authority to seek redress against external enemies (Declaration of War Against Western Civilization 2010). This shouldn't justify the violence used to achieve outcome (Smilansky 2010), especially if there is truth to the Golden Rule. Islamic Extremists believe that Allah is the ultimate authority. These effects are at risk of unintended and intended innocent casualties, but proportional in achieving their goals. When using Allah and the Declaration of War against Americans as the higher authority for terrorists, al-Qaeda is justified under the Just War tenants to conduct war. Al-Qaeda views all Americans and supporters of Western Civilization as enemies whether they are combatants, noncombatants, or citizens of the domestic society, and will take action to eliminate the world of evil. When using research to prove or disprove terrorism brings scary findings, but one matter stands true, life is cherished by all cultures regardless of religions.

To prove my research as life being cherished, Just Cause allows states to protect themselves from barbarians and ensure the safety or honor of allies (Christopher 2004). A last resort is when a public declaration is not honored by an ultimatum, and nothing else is available to lead to a peaceful resolution (Christopher 2004). Regardless of theories, none are established in doctrine, and it is truly a reflection of ethics of human beings. Cicero's Just War theory points out that killing is always wrong, but it is justified when states or governments are pursuing national interests. Terrorist groups are not governments or states, and religion is not being used in the manner intended to seek their achievements. Terrorism will exist as long as we are alive.

Military retaliation will place our society and many other peaceful societies in position of knowing violence, which means we only use brute force to borrow lunch money when we are hungry. Daily living will constantly become disturbed by military retaliation, just like terrorism places fear in all people throughout the world after evil attacks (American Psychological Association 2011). When examining the religious justifications for terrorism, I feel that the "end doesn't justify the means," or terrorism ideologies are not strong determinism in their Justified evil actions. Like many things throughout the world, people's beliefs from their culture are altered by pressure and money. Currently, the United States is threatened by terrorism and debt. The next chapter explains reasons for our debt.

We cannot become concerned with death while living, but we can die to live through the support of those we love and the knowing that there is more in life than who we are as individuals, there is a God; individuals must find that path to prove existence for themselves and not for others.

Chapter 16

IS THERE A STRUGGLE TO FEEL SECURE?

Freedom . . . What is freedom without feeling secured in your own home? The world is continuing to be threatened by terrorist activity and unexpected disasters that deeply traumatize people who experience such horrific events. The lack of effort in preventing terrorism leading to the terrorist attacks on September 11, 2001 and the failure to maintain levies in New Orleans after Hurricane Katrina led to disasters greater than the horrific events themselves, that being the emotional scarring of victims. The psychological wounds that victims, rescue workers, and children sustained cannot be healed in a day, but could take a lifetime to recover from. Whether there is an act of terrorism or a natural disaster, both kinds of events require attention toward the mental-health issues of the people who experienced trauma from them. This can be done by continuing to ensure that resources are available to victims and rescue workers and by limiting exposure to media, especially for victims who are children.

On August 29, 2005, Hurricane Katrina swept through New Orleans, Louisiana, early in the morning. New Orleans is below sea level and required levees to protect the land (Bourget 2005). It is fortunate that the storm itself did not threaten life. The storm turned for the worse when the levees broke (Bourget 2005). People were prepared for the hurricane and the federal government was prepared to assist New Orleans in hurricane response, but the breaking of the levees changed all aspects of emergency response and recovery due to massive flooding (Bourget 2005). The public required help, and the government reacted slowly to the unexpected conditions. Sadly, while the state was ready for a hurricane, it was failure in planning for the breaking of levees that caused such devastation (Bourget 2005). The United States government provided funds to ensure maintenance and additions were conducted on the levees, but the proper maintenance was not done (Bourget 2005). Communities wanted answers to the slow response, and continue to need more resources to assist them in mental health and medical recovery (Waters 2010). The death toll in Louisiana wasn't from the hurricane. It was due to flooding, and people are still recovering emotionally and continue to rebuild communities (Rhodes 2010).

Another situation that caused the American people to experience flooding of physical and emotional pain was the terrorist attacks of September 11, 2001. Eleven years ago, the world witnessed the attacks of the World Trade Centers. Many New York City goers watched the horrific events from the windows of their apartments. This tragedy brought caused emotional trauma due to the nature of incident as two jetliners crashed into the World Trade Center's Twin Towers. This introduced a new means of terrorism the world had never seen (Borum 2004). This terrorist event was escalated by Osama bin Laden's Declaration of War against Western Civilization (Borum 2004). The terrorist event increased security and placed law-enforcement agencies in a position to develop and change procedures to prevent or even react to terrorist activity so civil rights are not violated (Roper 2003). With safety in question, it will be difficult to balance the Constitutional rights of Americans and provide thorough security procedures that deter or prevent terrorist activity while preventing the spark of emotional pain on victims and society in general (Forest, n.a.).

Both the events of 9/11 and Hurricane Katrina share victims left with emotional pain they will have to deal with the rest of their lives. Hurricane Katrina had many effects on people: people lost their homes or spent weeks away from their homes, people lost family members, the economy broke at the knees as jobs were lost, and most people had to live in controlled environments like shelters. Hurricane Katrina caused many people to experience long-term mental-health issues. One area to consider is the time it took to be rescued. The longer someone were pending rescue, the greater the possibility of suffering more severely psychologically. Post Traumatic Stress Disorder (PTSD) and Chronic Stress symptoms are a result of the hurricane. The PTSD condition was a result of dead people lying in the open, and the constant fear of losing one's own life or losing a family member. Chronic Stress results from the state still recovering from the hurricane and the individual physical health of victims, which remain constant reminders of the event. Both these conditions led to victims and rescue workers becoming more irritable, arguments, and family discord, including domestic violence. Victims including children also act out and display aggressive behavior toward others due to their illness and psychosomatic problems. Two things that September 11 and Katrina had in common in the mental behaviors of victims and rescue workers are the increased alcohol consumption, increase substance abuse, and survivor's guilt (Dewart, Frank, and Schmeidler 2003).

September 11 terrorist attacks brought a new light on emotional pain once associated mostly with combat veterans of war. Both victims and rescue workers experienced PTSD and Acute Stress (Posttraumatic Stress Disorder 2003). A study reported in the August 7, 2002 issue of Journal of American Medical Association stated that 11 percent of New York City residents had PTSD from the attacks that took place on September 11, 2001 (Schlenger, Caddell, Ebert, and Jordan 2002). They have recurring thoughts or nightmares about the attacks, including trouble sleeping or a change in eating habits (Posttraumatic Stress Disorder 2003). Anxiety and fear are more likely, especially if they are exposed to events or situations reminiscent of the trauma (Posttraumatic Stress Disorder 2003). People who experienced 9/11 are more on edge daily and can be startled easily by others due to being in deep thought or depression. The depression also leads to low self-esteem and low energy that cause difficulty in memory. The loss of memory will ultimately bring problems in the workplace since the individual focus is consumed by fatigue. There can also be emotional numbness (Posttraumatic Stress Disorder 2003).

Resources for both disasters differ in many ways. Katrina's victims had to learn from their lessons, where New York had a system in place to support treatment and assist victims. New Orleans was prepared for the hurricane but not the floods. Under the National Strategy for Homeland Security, the Federal Emergency Management Agency and the Red Cross provided much-needed recovery efforts for New Orleans. The Red Cross was also dispatched with FEMA to assist Louisiana Health Department in recovery efforts (Office for Victim of Crimes, n.a.). This action was due to a federal response plan, which indicated federal support efforts during and after disasters. The Louisiana Health Department also had family-assistant services and centers, but they underestimated the number of victims (Silke 2003). The health-care system became crippled by the floods and lacked health care and counseling services. After the disaster, the family-services centers provide necessary information and counseling services to families that suffered or experience the disaster. Louisiana has dedicated much effort in providing resources to treat and assist victims and rescue workers through 125 Acute Care Facilities, 44 more rural hospitals being built, state level health care clinics, and more (Silke 2003). This devastation identified required improvements at a local and federal level.

New York City seemed to be more prepared than expected regarding the terrorist attacks. New York City had the Multi-Jurisdictional Multi-Hazard Mitigation Plan that the federal government recognized, but many emergency services provided immediate care when the attacks took place. The plan was prepared in response to the Disaster Mitigation Act (DMA) of 2000. DMA 2000 requires states and local governments to prepare all hazard mitigation plans in order to remain eligible to receive pre-disaster mitigation funds from the federal government in case disaster takes place. All New York State County Emergency Services honor the DMA 2000. It effectively improves the disaster planning toward hazard mitigation. In the same light, the Federal Emergency Management Agency also provides resources to victims of natural disasters under the same act. Another opportunity offered to the victims and rescue workers is crisis counseling for short and long-term mental-health conditions due to the DMA 2000; it led to $155 million in federal funds toward Project Liberty allowed for an infrastructure that supports the demands of treating large number of mental-health conditions, which led to successful collaboration in establishing mental health needs for special concerned population (Donahue 2006). Like Katrina, though, the magnitude of the disaster caused by the attacks was more than the project was prepared to handle.

Both New York and Louisiana made great strides in providing health-care services to a well-populated environment of mental-health illness, but both states need to plan for the future, as the long-term effects of these disasters will continue. It is difficult to believe that anyone who witnessed either or both disasters is not affected. Both events are considered large-scale disasters, and people exposed to these environments are likely to have mental illness. One of the first areas of assistance to exposed people is psychological first aid. This is supported care for the most affected victims. For rescue workers, rapid debriefing or discussion of incident is not recommended since it can cause other stressors to be identified. Pharmaceutical therapy and psychotherapy are best for long-term treatment for victims and rescue workers who suffer from PTSD, depression, acute stress, and chronic stress. State projects, programs, and federal assistance can only provide to those willing to be helped at the time all programs are offered. Mental health will always have challenges due to natural and manmade disasters, but victims will only go as far as programs and funding will allow. Mental-health facilities need to continue research and create plans for the long-term effects so proper treatment can be provided so victims cannot walk away while their lives are still in shambles.

Children who experienced the trauma of either Hurricane Katrina or the terrorist attacks of 9/11 were deeply affected. In New York City, the residents suffering from the attacks ranged from children to elderly folk, but the children were more affected by the attacks

(Schlenger, Caddell, Ebert, and Jordan 2002). There are many options for adults to seek assistance for mental-health conditions so their lives are not in shambles, but children don't have that freedom of choice as they presume that their experiences are the norm, or they are afraid to discuss feelings to prevent harassment. Children require much energy from care givers, if there was any neglect or maltreatment, this can affect the outcome of a disaster even further. Children heal from emotional wounds through time, not reminders; children are vulnerable to PTSD and will have anger issues later (Waters 2010). Children may need a relaxed family structured life that allows children to join parents in the bed at night. Children must be allowed to be children. Their routines should be kept a regular as possible. Parents need to maintain themselves first by not discussing issues and acting as if problems are present in the family because of a disaster. Children will remember, but parents have the responsibility to provide proper guidance in all aspects of a child's life.

In addition, the media can amplify information when disasters or terrorist attacks occur, but there are long-term effects on children who view all media resources. Natural-disaster and terrorist events are horrific to both children and adults, but children suffer the long-term effects since television and wireless products are the tools of today's nonsocial outlets for people. Technology has added prolonged conditions to children. Children's protective shield is disrupted by media and can cause underlining development issues (Pynoos, Steinberg, and Wraith 1995). Children are watching the destruction of terrorism when people's homes are destroyed. In the same coverage children are killed, which viewers start assuming emotional thoughts of "What If?" and speak of the matter as if they experienced the conditions first hand.

The media plays a powerful role as it provides information to the public. Information is the pipeline from which the community learns of events, and especially when terrorism is likely or a natural disaster occurred, the public will be glued to the media. The impact it has on individuals like children, victims, emergency responders, and the general public can agitate psychological symptoms. If the media delivers bad information, it can be distracting and destructive. For example, the events that took place after September 11, 2001 involved inaccurate stories provided by the media due to the mad rush of getting the story. This distracted first responders and brought unnecessary emotional pain to victims and families on edge due to the attacks on the World Trade Center (Aleshinloye 2011).

Another psychological effect that impacts individuals is the technology of today; it increases immediacy and emotional responses to include fear or anger. Images provided by the media can be disturbing. Allowing the general public to become possible reporters using wireless communication like cell phones, iphones and androids eyewitness reporting) poses a problem since authorities are not offered the opportunity to screen a broadcast for accuracy before it is reported. That can cause more fear in the community than necessary, spread rumors, and start errors of information. The media can magnify the importance of information more than necessary, and especially in the case of terrorism or natural disasters, victims should limit exposure to media to reduce psychological agitation. Add viewing experience with physical experience, and then the conditions multiply. The media is the information train of the world and must practice due regard when publishing news; the news can trigger the past memories of people who mentally suffered from terrorist attacks.

In conclusion, the failed emergency response during the flooding caused by Hurricane Katrina caused trauma for its victims. In addition, the terrorist attacks of 9/11 had a tremendous psychological impact on their victims. While the victims did have some resources available to them, they were not sufficient. As a result of these events, the government has changed emergency response procedures and created opportunities to render appropriate assistance. The emotional pain the victims, rescue workers, and children still experience from both Katrina and 9/11 needed efficiency for duration, not just patchwork. Both situations placed many people who experienced the events into emotional rollercoaster rides of acute and long-term distress, anxiety, anger, and depression beyond the ability of the public-health departments of either New York or Louisiana to treat. Children were severely affected by both disasters and also exhibit symptoms of trauma, which will take extensive resources and time to heal. Victims, rescue workers, and children will continue to struggle psychologically as the media disseminates headline reminders of news to the public in a hypercompetitive manner without regard of who could be watching. In addition, the situations mentioned in this chapter require money to aid toward recovery for people and infrastructure. To recover well from disaster requires a strong economy.

Ego Lane always intersects with Reality Drive. Be cautious of the drive-thru's on Ego Lane.

Chapter 17

WILL ECONOMIC CONCERNS PREVENT PROTECTION?

THIS CHAPTER DESERVES a separate book, but the information I provide is my opinion on the reasons America is struggling and will continue to struggle. The factors of economic concern identified by me are few and not all matters pertaining to our current debt. 2012 has past and there were tremendous financial concerns that led to military cuts, less emergency service personnel, and fewer public safety personnel. The time has come to back-step in spending. We are greedy as Americans. Our countries current economic recovery is becoming a financial strain to provide services that protect the public and national interests. I feel that there is one area that is needed to sustain protection of the United States: that is the housing market. I am not an expert in economics. Again, this is my opinion regarding the lack of funds available for protection in America.

This chapter may be challenging to follow as I cover many factors that threaten the 2013 and beyond economic recovery. If we have a strong housing market, we will sustain protection of America from terrorism and natural disaster. The housing market is up and then down, but terrorism is planned while natural disasters are random, but both have devastating results. Terrorism has placed governments in bad positions to allocate funds to allow more protection from terrorism and disaster aid response. A recession is in place, and the efforts to battle terrorism overseas and in the homeland are not aiding the process toward a strong economy on the home front, look how long it took to get money approved for hurricane Sandy. Regardless of the root cause, this is the longest recession in history, which leaves much concern for the future. We the American people are more vulnerable to attacks due to the nation's fiscal crisis. The secretary of the Treasury and chairperson of the Federal Reserve must take every effort to place the United States on the track toward recovery. Moreover, the United States needs to be sure that the established fiscal policy is appropriate toward long-term recovery.

Our recovery effort and established policies must implement a plan. Some factors to consider that created the recession were Americans buying property over their available means and excessive land regulations. Both of these factors drove the direction of the market. Going back to the first cause, profligate lending prior to the Bush Administration by itself did not cause the disaster of the financial crisis (Guina 2008). It was aided by the land restrictions toward development. This caused mortgage rates to rise higher than expected during the Bush Administration. This was no longer a traditional market. The housing market created the most severe crisis since the Great Depression (Guina 2008). The mortgage market was undermined and led to the failure of firms like Bear Sterns and Lehman Brothers, and the virtual failures of Fannie Mae and Freddie Mac (Cox 2008). This type of failure affected the world economy. Paul Krugman mentioned, "That smart growth, property consolidation in urban and metropolitan environments, is the single leading cause of our housing market bubble" (Cox 2008). Smart growth caused a demand for housing, which raised mortgage rates in most urban and metropolitan areas of the United States. Smart growth is the expansion of urban sprawls. The urban sprawls impacted mortgage rates. Places that were not affected by mortgage rates were ultimately affected by ration rates. Another contributing factor to high mortgages is population. Our population has grown four times more since 2000 (Cox 2008). Population alone drives a serious demand. People want food and a place to hang the hat. Many believe that the current financial crisis would not have occurred without the profligate lending that became pervasive in the United States. "Land use rationing policies of smart growth clearly intensified the problem and turned what may have been a relatively minor downturn into a global financial meltdown" (Cox 2008).

This type of problem in America did not get there overnight, even though it feels that way. There are people we need to identify as key actors of the recession. I believe them to be President George W. Bush and the United States Congress, but they had a war and homeland security matters that required full effort. The country is more in debt by war and homeland security. Prior to President Bush, President Bill Clinton introduced affordable means for owning a home. In 2008, President Bush addressed the nation regarding the economy (New York Times 2008). Based on President Bush's address to the nation regarding the economy in 2008, he obviously understood the depth of his decisions in office and the impact made on the country. During President Bush's presidency, the stock market tripled, financial institutions failed, banks restricted lending, and private businesses had difficulty borrowing money.

Due to President Clinton's affordable mortgages, bank lenders were complacent during the Bush Administration and failed to conduct checks and balance on individuals applying for loans. President Bush's speech mentioned that he didn't know the root cause of our current crisis, but later identified how mortgages have lost value and banks have restricted money (New York Times 2008). One thing is for sure: it took time to get to this point within the country economically. My concern is that our government is bouncing from one major problem to another, causing much red tape to be confused with or forgotten while soothing the economy and battling terrorism.

Terrorism will never be resolved! President Obama is still handling the war on terrorism and seeking resolution of the financial crisis while the deficit continues to grow, to include a gas crisis which continues to go up and then down. Current and future President's have much to consider on all factors mentioned in this chapter and book since the topics are concerning while securing America. To prove that terrorism is causing problems within the financial market, Senate Banking Committee Chairman Christopher Dodd (D-Conn) mentioned, "that reform would have to wait on current crisis" (Kane 2009). The National Consumer Law Center and the National Association of Consumer Advocates are arguing the holdup and emphasized patience on the Housing and Economy Recovery Act of 2008, because it will cause more damage to the economy. In the meantime, 5.4 million mortgages are delinquent, or foreclosed and home prices continue to fall (Kane 2009).

The Housing and Economic Recovery Act was developed to heal with the wounds created from the 2006–2007 high levels of defaults and foreclosures among residence mortgages (Knapp 2009). Two thousand eight doubled the previous recorded high. From 2008 to the current date, it seems to continue to rise with no light at the end of the tunnel, even though rates are awesome now during 2012 and beginning of 2013. The level of foreclosures and prime fixed-rate loans will continue to burden the financial crisis. This means the Home Ownership and Equity Act of 1994 will not work with today's consumer. In July 2008, Congress approved and authorized the Federal Housing Administration, under Housing and Economic Recovery Act of 2008, to insure (Insurance) up to $300 billion in loans via a new program: HOPE for Home Owners (Kane 2009). Congress is attempting to make amendments to increase participation in the program (Collins 2009). This should provide an opportunity for families to own a home. So far, this program has not worked well, and the money could have been of more benefit spent on security operations for the homeland. As a result, Congress made new effort to encourage loan modifications as part of its Making Homes Affordable plan on February 18, 2009 (Collins 2009). Since that change, realtors try not to offer the opportunity to families since the plan will not keep them in the home due to the 31 percent interest rate and principle. This proves the program is insufficient, which will eventually lead to a new plan causing more shortcomings to the current mortgage crisis.

Speaking of shortcomings, let's look at the lack of bank management and Department of Treasury's involvement in savings banks. They took risks hoping that the government would bail the banks out of trouble, but that failed as banks disappeared at the fast rate of a hundred per quarter at the beginning of 2009. The Department of the Treasury is limited on what actions it can take by the Federal Reserve Act. This should prevent the next Great Depression, but the Treasury in October 2008 supported Mitsubishi's $9 Billion investment in Morgan Stanley (Kane 2009). The Treasury insured that the investment in Morgan Stanley would not be diluted in the future (Kane 2009). This promise should have never been given for such an investment. This is also the turning of the clock when the United States government got involved with banking before the depression of 1930s. In addition, this action "prevents private sector resolution as new equity is less likely attempted to arbitrage the initial fire sale" (Knapp 2009). Today, the Treasury is still getting involved with banks. Bank of America never formalized the asset insurance contract (Knapp 2009). The Treasury bargained with Bank of America to identify eligibility for insurance, what fees were payable, and the amount of the first-loss so Bank of America could recover (Collins 2009). This type of activity should be handled at an analogous level that achieves management of monetary policy (Collins 2009). It seems that Treasury is making more decisions than expected, which leads to debates of handling monetary policy. The secretary of Treasury at the time, Hank Paulson, should have prevented this bank recovery from being completed. This type of deal pushes the Federal Reserve System, America's Central Bank, further than permitted by Congress and will later show the way toward bank failure, even if it were poor bank management. The Federal Reserve has no control of the current recession. Two thousand and seven was identified as the highest recession in history, but 2011 has met that same high and continue rising in rates (Collins 2009). The Federal Reserve should not have any political relation, regardless of who is elected by the president. This would prevent America being manipulated by money or placed into a financial crisis.

Prior to 2003, our country started feeling the financial crisis. Due to the crisis the Federal Reserve (Fed) approved sub-prime lending, which later created more complications in 2003 (Collins 2009). From 2003 to 2006 the Fed had a difficult time deciding rates when the housing market proved to be in difficult standings. During this time, rates were lowered by the Fed in efforts to intrigue the interest in buyers, but America was still in need for housing (Collins 2009). It is the Fed's responsibility to prevent this. There are examiners in the Fed that read and react, in a balanced and effective manner, to symptoms of problems that may not yet be obvious to the bank world. The problem the country is facing is the hold- up by Congress to fix this crisis. The Department of Treasury and the Federal Reserve must create a team of people who can intervene and start regulating the condition. If intervention works, without inducing excessive spending, our economic quantity will be properly evaluated to our economic fluctuations in the financial system (Italiano 2009). The economy will recover slowly, but the concern with this is the monetary value we will require to stabilize the economic crisis. The policies for the monetary must be strong, but the dream team brought in to fulfill this obligation can either make it work or make the country economic crisis worse.

The market plays a major role when understanding the monetary. Monetary policy in the United States has an extreme history, but we need to only identify the importance and effect of it during the last twelve years. President Bush knew the crisis that stood in front of him, but no realistic actions were taken except for spending more money than planned by the Federal Reserve. Depending who is selling the pitch, some speculators claim that the recession started in 2007 while others claim in early 1990s while President Clinton was in office (Italiano 2009). It is not important who was in office when turmoil of the financial market occurred. Essentially, the recession started in 2007, but the financial crisis began in 2003.

From 2003 to 2006 the federal funds rate was well below what we experienced during the previous two decades of good economic macroeconomic performance (Auerbach and Gale 2009). The Fed policy supported this, and it was a contributor to the "Great Moderation" period of this country. According to Investopedia. com, Great Moderation is the name given to the period of decreased macroeconomic volatility experienced in the United States (Investopedia.com, n.a.). In addition, during this period, the standard deviation of quarterly real Gross Domestic Product (GDP) declined by half, and the standard deviation of inflation declined by two-thirds (Auerbach and Gale 2009).

With this in mind, such a decline means we are in the worst GDP decline since the 1980s. We just keep going back in time regarding American history. In the 1930s, the Great Depression affected the country longer than it should have because of the Fed's weak enforcement of a non-aggressive approach. It is happening today as the "real estate bubble" will continue to have good moments and bad moments, but nothing sustained or stable (Auerbach and Gale 2009). I believe it can be sustained since there are funds being established supposedly to support the country in 2006, but the raised rate of 5.25 percent placed America into recession (Auerbach and Gale 2009). This brings the country into the 2007 to 2009 improvement process. The purpose of the Fed is to cut rates, not raise rates when the country is drowning.

In support of the Fed position, there was an attempt to drop the rate, but the attempt failed because the market was not responding. This placed the Fed to "take further action and possibly cause Fiscal Policy to change" (Auerbach and Gale 2009). Change did take place; everything halted. During the recession there were unforeseen challenges that faced the monetary discretionary fiscal policy (Auerbach and Gale 2009). The fiscal policy will continue to change each fiscal year due to the 0.5 discount factor that leads to variables being scaled by the GDP (Auerbach and Gale 2009). Two thousand nine was the year of many changes like the stimulus package in February 2009. It appeared that 2009 was very aggressive in policies, when in reality policy could have been less aggressive to achieve more results. I mention this because many plans were developed, but not one seems well thought out, but it can be too early to evaluate.

It seems that the 2009 stimulus will not work for years to come. However, there are ideas to create an "automatic stabilizer" through taxes (Auerbach and Gale 2009). This is the plan from the Obama Administration, even though the most consideration is on the macroeconomic effects. Long-term worries will determine whether or not the stabilizer will be effective in the United States. My concern is that the common timeline for the Fed forecast models toward economic development could even take effect is two years. Tax changes did take place in 2009, 2010, 2011, and currently 2012 when the Obama Administration made efforts to improve economic activity overall (Auerbach and Gale 2009). More taxes mean more money from the American people when their salaries are decreasing. For example, the military personnel got a 1.3 percent pay increase in 2009 when the country rose at 3.9. That means military service members got a cut, not a raise. This type of taxation led business management to difficult times.

Business in America is more important than one might imagine, especially when business and investments go hand in hand. One change that should be estimated is the response of business in fixed investment with incentives (Auerbach and Gale 2009). This is difficult to establish due to "fewer natural experiments" that analyze the investment front and poor tax provisions (Auerbach and Gale 2009). If the Obama Administration continues to change policies, the business world will feel the effect in multiple fashions when long-term recovery plans change every two years. Two years is not long-term. It is enough time to see a plan come into effect, but not enough time to prove its credibility.

With the future being undetermined by the financial world, current policies have proven to neglect all aspects of the economy. Regardless of the past traditional market, in today's world, the Fed and the presidential administration need to take an aggressive stance to protect America so homes are affordable, rates are acceptable, and national debt isn't the daily focus that threat taxes which lead to cuts in military power and public services. As I have already mentioned, the population is growing and so are the demands for day-to-day life needs. This is causing more Americans to look for more than one job or seek alternatives to supply their families' basic needs. Money equals manpower in the military and public service jobs. Manpower equals more means in tending to terrorism prevention measures and disaster relief aid. Military strength and personnel required for emergency services or public safety will not be achieved without a strong economy. Money is not the only area that hinders proactive protection; laws and policies can do the same.

My time as a subordinate made me feel as if I could lead or charge others in greater abilities than those above me; my time as a leader educated me on being a fine subordinate.

Chapter 18

DOES RED TAPE PREVENT PROACTIVE MEASURES?

Engaging subordinates and leaders in person is leadership;
passion for duty shows quality of compassion. This is a must to
support fellow comrades that sweat achieving mission required
tasks daily.

WITH TERRORISM BEING a constant topic in the United States, one may
wonder if there is any hope to preserve humanity and human rights
within the United States. Additional concerns are also directed to
the active shooting situations that occurred nationwide, such as the
Colorado Movie Theater shooting, and Newtown Connecticut. Terrorism
and active shootings have made society, emergency responders, and
active duty military service members more vulnerable. There are only
approximately 450, 000 police officers nationwide, not all in patrol
status, protecting the American streets, but they are consumed with
the daily domestic responses that take them away from the proactive
policing that many perceive is being conducted. Between terrorism
and active shooting situations, 450, 000 officers of the law are not
enough.

How do police officers become the eyes and ears of their
communities when they can't fulfill the routine community policing,
because of the large volume of calls one patrol officer responds to

daily? The short answer is they cannot, especially since they must write, review, and correct reports in the midst of their shift work. With all the red tape of laws and policies, there must be an easier approach in achieving proactive response and reporting to acts of terrorism and active shootings to save life or lives.

This is a disturbing thought since there are many citizens who have qualifying training in firearms that hold positions deemed as law-enforcement compatible, but are not granted the authority outside their official jurisdictions. This refers to military police, all Department of Defense police, Coast Guard, military and DoD explosive ordnance disposal specialists, military and DoD correctional cross-country chasers, all military level branch security forces that protect nuclear locations, DoD defensive drivers, and embassy security guards of American interests. Why can't these people perform their duties outside their official jurisdictions? When presenting such a powerful question, the easy response by many is the Posse Comitatus Act of 1878, yet this act is vague.

In my research, I discovered *The Origins of the Posse Comitatus* by Bonnie Baker, written in November 1999, in which she identifies the origins better than most. The approval of original Posse Comitatus came in 1878 under Chapter 263, section 15 (Baker 1999). It identified the army, during that time as Posse Comitatus, which means the army of the United States cannot enforce laws unless events were to take place in the United States that would authorize it to under the Constitution or by act of Congress (Baker 1999). The objective or intent of Chapter 263, section 15, did not expect military forces to expand into different branches, and different occupation within the branches.

Military personnel in occupational specialties in public service, i.e. Police, Fire, Explosives Disposal, and more are threatened by Chapter 263, section 15, which keeps trained individuals from protecting our homeland. What is ironic, I asked a group of people at a coffee shop, "What if specially trained people from the military or DoD were allowed to carry concealed firearms in off duty status?" I was appalled at the response. They replied that military members are too young and irresponsible to carry such responsibility. I asked if any of them wished to be police officers, and one did. The age of the prospect was twenty. He was currently attending a part-time police academy at Palomar College, in California, which is one year long. That would make him twenty-one when he graduates from the academy and eligible to become a police officer for any agency that is hiring.

According to Baker, "Sec. 375 Restriction on direct participation by military personnel, and the Secretary of Defense shall prescribe such regulation as maybe necessary to ensure that any activity (including the provision of any equipment of facility or the assignment or detail of any personnel) under this chapter doesn't include or permit direct participation by a member of the Army, Navy, Air Force, or Marine Corps in a search, seizure, arrest, or other similar activity unless participation in such activity by such member is otherwise authorized by law" (Baker 2003), but Title 10, Subtitle A, Part 1 of Chapter 18 of the United States Code (USC) mentions different, which makes the Posse Comitatus Act that more diluted. I mention in this chapter the possibility of military support for civilian law enforcement agencies.

If I were a police chief of any agency, I would be intimidated to even ask the local military police agency to "back one of my officers," this means support of any law enforcement officer in the performance of their duties when alone. As an Augment MP, I always backed an officer on a traffic stop conducted on Interstate-5 (I-5 runs through Camp Pendleton) or stayed near the area until he was "Code 4." Code 4 means conditions and safety are not in question, situation under control. In turn, I conducted a traffic stop on Camp Pendleton and was backed by a California Highway Patrolman (CHP) who was on base picking up a police report for one of his cases. Are we wrong for doing the right thing for officer safety? Do local jurisdictions and military-police jurisdictions have a right to have a Memorandum of Agreement per 32 CFR 637.4, Military Police and the USACIDS, in order to support one another? In addition, if something was to go wrong, I have immediate support that means the difference between life and death.

Why are DoD police struggling to get H.R. 675 approved? Under chapter 18, the United States Coast Guard is granted law-enforcement authority for individuals trained in law enforcement, so why shouldn't MPs and the civilian counter-parts (DoD civilian police) of all branches of the military be added to the same provisions of law? In fact, an MP can support civilian law enforcement and vice versa, only when violations of law are being investigated that pertain to the Constitution of the United States. The Constitution is derived from the base of principles and laws that protect the reasonability of society. If drivers average fifty-five miles per hour on a certain road, *prima facia*, when someone is way under or over that limit, it is a violation. It is the responsibility of law-enforcement officers in their jurisdictions to ensure laws are enforced to prevent society from abusing rights and freedoms. Both entities have the same mission in different jurisdictions, and all law enforcement agencies need more simplified regulations in efforts to assist each other. One team, one fight.

There are too many regulations that limit all law-enforcement agencies. From the beginning of the book, I have discussed the tools available for law enforcement to protect the United States pertaining to terrorism, but everything regarding Posse Comitatus is dated before the terrorist events unfolded on September 11, 2001. There is more, especially when combining efforts of the military. We already notice the convoluted writing of the Posse Comitatus Act, and there is more. Here they are:

1) 10 USC 331-334. (Civil Disturbance Statutes).

2) 42 USC 5121, (the Stafford Act).

3) 44 CFR Part 206, Federal Emergency Management Agency.

4) AR 500-50, Civilian Disturbances, 21 Apr 1972.

5) AR 500-51, Support to Civilian Law Enforcement, 1 Aug 1983.

6) AR 700-131, Loan and Lease of Army Materiel, 4 Sep. 1987.

7) CJCS Instruction 3710.01A, DoD counter Drug Operational Support, 23 Apr 1997.

8) CJCS Instruction 3121.01, Standing Rules of Engagement for US Forces, 1 Oct. 1994.

9) DoD Civil Disturbance Plan ("Garden Plot"), Feb 1991.

10) DoD Dir. 3025.1, Military Support to Civil Authorities, 15 Jan 1993.

11) DoD Dir. 3025.12, Military Assistance to Civil Disturbances (MACDIS), 4 Feb 1994.

12) DoD Dir. 3025.15, Military Assistance to Civil Authorities, 18 Feb 1997.

13) DoD Manual 3025.1M, Manual for Civil Emergencies, Jun 1994.

14) DoD Dir. 5525.5, DoD Cooperation with Civilian Law Enforcement Officials.

15) DoD Dir. 5525.10, Using Military Working Dog Teams to Support Law Enforcement Agencies in Counter-drug Missions, 17 Nov. 1990.

16) FM 19-15, Civil Disturbances, 25 Nov 1985.

17) FM 100-19, Domestic Support Operations, Jul 1993.

18) Joint Pub 3-07.4, Joint Counter-drug Operations, 17 Feb. 1998.

19) NAVMC 2915, Counter-drug Campaign Plan, 23 Nov. 1993.

20) NGR 500-2/ANGI 10-801, National Guard Counter-drug Support to Law Enforcement.

21) MCO 3000.8B, Employment of Marine Corps Resources in Civil Disturbances, 30 Jul 1979.

22) MCO 3440.7, Marine Corps Ass't to Civil Authorities, 1 Jan 1992.

These are not all aspects pertaining to the topic; this is only a minimal list to give an example of how local law-enforcement jurisdictions and judges can easily be confused or make the wrong decision regarding military and civil-law enforcement interaction. Legal firms, police departments, and district attorneys need to have a military specialist to aid in the decision process when circumstances require military aid. To help simplify the understanding of Posse Comitatus, "Posse" means a body of men. "Comitatus" means the summons to enforce the law. An MP is an individual in a law-enforcement capacity, not an infantryman raiding the streets with his posse.

Through research of the Posse Comitatus Act, I found a number of good articles that aid more understanding. I recommend that you read the following articles on the matter:

(1) Cronin, R.B. (n.d.). *Military Support to Civilian Law Enforcement Agencies.* United States Marine Corps, Headquarters, Washington, D.C. Retrieved from https://www.ncjrs.gov/pdffiles1/Digitization/130308NCJRS.pdf

(2) Probst, J. (n.d.). *The Posse Comitatus Act: What Does It Mean to Local Law Enforcement?* United States Air Force, 90th Missile Security Force Squadron, F. E. Warren Air Force Base. Retrieved from http://www.policechiefmagazine.org/magazine/index.cfm?fuseaction=display_arch&article_id=335&issue_id=72004

(3) Kopel, D., and P. Blackan, P. (n.d.). *Can Soldiers Be Peace Officers.* Retrieved from http://www.constitution.org/2ll/2ndschol/134kbm.pdf

(4) Lauve, R. (1983). *Military Cooperation with Civilian Law Enforcement Agencies.* United States General Accounting Office, Washington, D. C. Retrieved from http://archive.gao.gov/d40t12/122004.pdf

Posse Comitatus and additional laws governing the use of military troops in the enforcement of civil laws is a collage of abilities the military can provide as a posse, but not mentioning the capabilities that law enforcement agencies within the military spectrum can provide. This is conflicting and confusion when there are different opinions or beliefs on the use of military troops in a peace-officer capacity. It is understood why Posse Comitatus is under direct authority of the president of the United States in efforts to maintain order in the streets of America when there is public disorder, but the act should not prevent all law-enforcement agencies from carrying out the responsibilities of protecting Americans, regardless of agency jurisdiction. A cop is a cop! All law-enforcement agencies have the inherent right, regardless of identity, to protect America. Protection of America, especially terrorism prevention, can be as simple as a traffic stop conducted by a police officer.

Why can't we allow military police, all Department of Defense police, coast guard, military and Defense explosive ordnance disposal specialists, military and Defense correctional cross-country chasers, all military level branch security forces that protect nuclear locations, Defense defensive drivers, and embassy security guards be allowed the same right as civilian law enforcement under H.R. 218, especially when the United States government allows for Executive Order 12425, which grants immunity to international criminal police organizations? Wouldn't Americans rather have people they know and trust with known training to be extra eyes and ears within the public, not international criminal police organizations? Having skilled and trusted Americans with "due right" under conditions of "due regard" may save lives in a school, movie theater, church, or place of prayer. Example, when an active shooting situation takes place or when that one vehicle-borne improvised explosive device attempts attack, there is someone qualified to react against the threat.

Here are more Red Tape items to consider in terrorism prevention:

Section 314, The U.S. PATRIOT Act (Uniting and Strengthening America by Providing Appropriate Tools Required to Intercept and Obstruct Terrorism), improved the process by which federal law-enforcement officials obtain legal authority for conducting surveillance and allowed for greater information sharing between criminal investigators and intelligence collectors. The act modified the definition of terrorism as a federal crime to include several offenses likely to be committed by terrorists, including specific computer crimes and a number of violent crimes involving aircraft. This increased list of federal offenses include attacks on mass-transportation systems, vehicles, facilities, or passengers; harboring or concealing persons who have committed or are about to commit an act of terrorism; expansion of the prohibition against providing material support or resources to terrorists, and possessing a biological agent or toxin of a type or in a quantity that is not reasonably justified for specifically defined purposes.

Section 311, International Money Laundering Abatement and Financial Anti-Terrorism Act of 2001was added into the US Patriot Act, which significantly increased the United States' ability to combat the financing of terrorism.

Section 313, October 29, 2001, President Bush issued Homeland Security Presidential Directive Number Two (HSPD-2). HSPD-2 offers federal guidance for keeping foreign terrorists and their supporters out of the United States through denial of entry, removal, and prosecution.

One of the most effective weapons in preventing terrorist attacks involves gathering, analyzing, and disseminating intelligence and the full integration of that intelligence into investigations, operations, and crisis response. Everything requires time for law enforcement to piece together a case. It is becoming harder for them to concentrate on more than one case at one time due to policies, regulations, and new laws. Policy makers or those that finalize laws need to consider the complications a law-enforcement professional has in pursuing more case loads when one case will require many hours and much effort that takes them away from additional cases that could be discovered.

If federal law enforcement and local law-enforcement agencies could pursue more cases, they could better prevent terrorist attacks like the one Jose Padilla attempted in 2002. This was an intriguing case. He was arrested and charged with planning a "Dirty Bomb" attack against the United States. Padilla was one of many detained after September 11, 2001 attacks. He was held in Navy custody with no charges and no access to counsel since he was being held as an enemy combatant. Federal Judge Michael Mukasey had many questions regarding Padilla's charges, and he ruled that Padilla could see a lawyer, even though he had planned to detonate a radioactive bomb in the United States. The United States government argued against the ruling it since the interrogation by the lawyer could be considered compromising. He was considered a critical intelligence source. It was a legal battle between the government and Judge Mukasey. As you can see, the US Patriot Act was used by authorities and frowned upon by the courts. The FBI knew of Padilla's conversion to Islam and that he provided information to al-Qaeda, and in turn al-Qaeda gave him cash and information on making bombs. According to the US Patriot Act, Padilla should have been watched, but the United States Constitution under the decision of the Judge Mukasey released him.

The safety of America is everything. Many question the civil liberties as law enforcement attempts to prevent or mitigate future terrorism. What would history say on the topic? Let's mix current terrorism threat that the executive branch is dealing with and thoughts of Benjamin Franklin. Soup to nuts; Americans continue to question their safety due to terrorism, they seem to have their own interpretation of the Fourth Amendment due to the US Patriot Act of 2001. The Patriot Act was created through checks and balances as expedient as possible due to the terrorist actions on September 11, 2001. These actions have changed the international security perspective, and protecting America was taken to the next level through the Patriot Act.

Preventing terrorism or crimes leading to terrorism is a growing concern as Americans question the means law enforcement is taking. One of the most effective weapons in the prevention of terrorist attacks involves the gathering, analysis, and dissemination of intelligence. This aids the process of collection of intelligence into investigations, operations, and crisis response. If Benjamin Franklin was still alive and witnessing the events, he would agree that protecting the foundation of America was imperative. I mention this since he stated in 1787 when the Constitution was approved, "Thus, I consent, sir, to this Constitution because I expect no better, and because I am not sure that it is not the best." I believe he stated this knowing that evolution is in front of society, not behind. This evolution leads to strategy and capabilities.

Prior to today's terrorism tactics, there is a longer history of terrorism as explained in earlier chapters. Biological and chemical uses such as poisoning wells, using powerful herbs, and infected corpses predate the use of gunpowder and explosives, and there is concern today that those historic weapons will be used again. Biological terrorism and attacks similar to the recent attacks of flying airplanes into buildings pose a threat of terrorism that affects all communities both nationally and internationally. The executive branch and all law-enforcement agencies want to keep America safe, while not violating civil rights. My definition: Violence or threat of violence generally directed against humanity (Reasonable Person) targets with the motives of political, and actions generally carried out in a way that will achieve maximum publicity that supports a perpetrators membership of an organized group, and, unlike other criminals.

Terrorist acts are intended to produce effects beyond the immediate physical damage they cause by having long-term psychological repercussions on a particular target audience. The fear created by terrorists, for example, may be intended to cause people to exaggerate the strength of the terrorists and the importance of their cause, to provoke governmental overreaction, to discourage dissent, or simply to intimidate and thereby enforce compliance with their demands.

Why are those who seek to serve their community become soiled by policy when attempting to protect mankind; in turn, this causes emergency-service personnel to fear every move or word made.

Chapter 19

WRAPPING IT UP

Passion comes in two fashions, one that is deemed to impress others of your ability, and the second being the use of your ability for others to succeed.

AMERICAN VALUES ARE being threatened by surrounding circumstances discussed in this book. Our efforts to be strong during hard times will continue to be challenged by terrorism. Preventing, countering, and even fighting terrorism is a long-term difficulty that changes our current American social and economic cultures. Each chapter reflects pieces of research to prove my theory that we are changed forever socially and economically due to terrorism. After reading this book I recommend reading *Because They Hate*, by Brigitte Gabriel, and *More Than a Carpenter*, by Josh McDowell and Sean McDowell, and a pamphlet *Islam and Christianity*, by Rev. Bruce Green. Please also view the series of videos, *The Third Jihad*, by Clarion Fund Inc, on You Tube:

1. Part 1- http://www.youtube.com/watch?v=ZZHnfFLZ9XU

2. Part 2 - http://www.youtube.com/watch?v=YbnaWpSS8Dk&feature=related

3. Part 3 - http://www.youtube.com/watch?v=m1d0Lx8MPtI&fea
   ture=related

4. Part4 - http://www.youtube.com/watch?v=QZdhKcFk5vg&feat
   ure=related

You can't always believe what you find on the Internet, but once you have completed your research, you can come to your own conclusions about what the books and videos discuss. We can always learn from one another as long as we research and analyze the material appropriately and support it with scholarly feedback. Is there more to terrorism? Yes. Why do *Third Jihad* and terrorism, and fear of either discussion cause so much red tape in protecting mankind? If we as Americans understood all aspects of Arab nations from culture to religion, we may approach matters more or less aggressively politically.

I believe the center of such threats presented by terrorism lies in the history of Hezbollah. Hezbollah is considered to be the world's strongest and most trained terrorist organization. Iran supports Hezbollah. Hezbollah originally started as Shi'a Islamic groups in 1982 within Lebanon. This group took credit for the bombing of the US Marine barracks in Beirut in 1983, the kidnapping of United States embassy officials in Beirut in 1984, hijackings in 1985, and the bombing of the Khobar Towers in 1996. Hezbollah is a strong organization that is highly disciplined and capable of sophisticated attacks around the world. The members are good at blending into society by working normal jobs within hospitals, media, and the education system. Their goal is the elimination of all Western civilization and its influences from their region. Hezbollah's primary goal is the destruction of Israel.

This is frightening, yet could this all be true? The Hezbollah structure seems to support this, since it is highly supported by Iran. They have military similarities in ranks and equipment but pursue goals best as immigrants in other countries. Hezbollah participates in tobacco smuggling, immigration fraud, and money laundering. Perhaps you may now understand why I have discussed the many topics that support, build, or profit terrorism cells. The Hezbollah hierarchy is based in Lebanon of a Shiite theocracy, similar to Iran. These organizations and many alike have mastered cell operations to achieve their goals.

Preventing terrorism cells from operating depends on United States policy and assistance from America's allies. The United States' counter terrorism strategies and the United States' support of Israel will have peaceful resolution if the relations never become broken. Israel has proven to be a master at counterterrorism, and all law-enforcement personnel in America need training in terrorism awareness. This training would also aid law-enforcement officials in investigation methods of petty crimes, which is important since terrorism organizations participates in petty crimes such as insurance fraud, credit card fraud, and many more that allow the group to blend into normal society. Counter terrorism strategies must limit cyber space access and screen all operating cells and suspected people linked to fraud detection. Counterterrorism needs to be dedicated to identifying specific terrorists, indicators of terrorism, and defined threats to America and to understanding the movement of people in possible terrorist groups before determining terrorism. Under Federal Code, 28 C.F.R., Judicial Administration, terrorism is "the unlawful use of force and violence against persons or property to intimidate or coerce a government, the civilian population, or any segment thereof, in further of political or social objectives" (Cornell Law website 2012). Terrorist organizations attempt to undermine the morale of the public so society can collapse from within America and Americans overseas. Terrorists thrive on the economy, public transportation, education systems, and community elections. Blending into society allows the usual activity to be ignored.

Terrorist organizations conduct operations of both high value and low value. To date, no American can explain the extreme ideology of terrorism. The motivation of terrorism has no limits. The Federal Bureau of Investigation is the hub and operational control for federal intelligence and law-enforcement activities against domestic terrorism. The FBI is responsible for the National Joint Terrorist Task Force.

International responsibility is placed on the Central Intelligence Agency, which reports directly to the president of the United States on any matter that threatens American interests or national security. The CIA has a counterterrorism role as it collects information internationally. Both agencies, to include many others mentioned in earlier chapters throughout this book, require information sharing with federal, local, and international law-enforcement agencies. This allows the FBI to keep close relations, but it is traditionally assumed that intelligence agencies monitor or track terrorist activity. The CIA makes great effort in human Intel (HUMIT) to prevent espionage. Both the FBI and CIA work together in counterterrorism efforts in attempts to prevent foreign and domestic terrorism threats. Anything outside the borders of the United States requires much discussion and review between international officials and United States Department of State officials. There are approxamately187 United States embassies, consulates, and legations overseas that support information collection to assist the Department of State in maintaining diplomacy. Like many agencies in the United States, money and manpower are the keys to success.

Both the FBI and the CIA can improve if personnel increases, but as Chapter 17 in this book discusses, personnel equals money, and there is very little available. The FBI may be the hub of law-enforcement information and antiterrorism activity, but it falls short when it comes to sourcing information quickly because it needs more personnel. Homeland Security has captured that realm, and it needs to respect the responsibilities being relinquished. The FBI handles white-collar crimes well. Clandestine operations in the CIA are exceptional; they employ skilled individuals with psychology and military training backgrounds to collect and pass information that can manipulate others. I believe that these agencies have true patriots attempting to stay ahead of the unpredictable beast of terrorism.

Before going any further, it is important to understand the difference between counterterrorism and antiterrorism. Counterterrorism is often mixed with antiterrorism, but they are very different yet they can also easily overlap each other. Counterterrorism is a strategic method that requires timely predictions through accurate intelligence. It provides proper warning and identifies whether a threat is serious or minimal. Counterterrorism is truly information that allows law-enforcement and military officials to act quickly to prevent attacks. Ultimately, the goal of both counterterrorism and antiterrorism is to prevent terrorist acts, reduce vulnerabilities to terrorism, and minimize damages from attacks. Antiterrorism does not rely on intelligence; it focuses on the physical security of potential targets such as embassies, military bases, nuclear power plants, etc. Counterterrorism is a large arena of responsibility, especially before events take place. After a terrorist attack, most people feel that it is more an emergency-management problem. That is not correct. Counterterrorism continues, but it is then identified as crisis management, depending on jurisdiction terminology. From my experience, counterterrorism is the following:

Counterterrorism is—Prediction through intelligence warning and mitigation by preparing proper authorities to stop an attack or protect critical infrastructures.

Antiterrorism is—Deterrence by hardening facilities considered possible targets, and prevention or detection through educating authorities on what to identify so proper report and action can be immediate.

Antiterrorism can be something that all agencies can adopt and teach within basic and advanced academies, some police agencies are doing that as we speak. They call it terrorism liaison officer training. This is a great strategy for local police departments to utilize. State and federal agencies can tackle the counterterrorism strategy, but manpower will always be a challenge and local police agencies would be requested by federal government to add law enforcement officers to a counterterrorism task force. Counterterrorism function in the global war on terror requires law enforcement and military readiness capability.

Readiness and capability can be initiated toward the individual threat or multiple threats that terrorism presents. Either way, it is truly intelligence and resources that aid officials. Many federal agencies and military identities comprise the counterterrorism community, but the jurisdiction where the incident takes place will have ultimate authority. Determining which strategy is best for today's global war on terrorism will always depend on the enemy we are fighting and the location we are fighting in. In the continental United States we should use all aspects of counterterrorism, but counterterrorism efforts overseas require more. The enemy has the upper hand overseas because of diplomacy and international law. We have to trust our allies to react quickly to terrorism. Our allies in turn must trust that we will cooperate in assisting them with counterinsurgency operations. Iraq is a small example of important things missed or pursued slowly because of politics and red tape. In Iran's case, just like Iraq, there has been too much time discussing policy to restrict a nation from performing inhumane developments that could threaten world peace.

In many cases the little stuff is being missed as in the case of Jordan. Jordan was established by a long history of Jewish and Muslim peace by King Abdullah bin al-Hussein. During the 1960s, peace turned in a different direction. Jordan was attacked and defeated by Israel in 1967. This defeat created much change in the region; the west bank was taken from Jordan, but Egypt, Jordan, and Syria were going to use conventional war to overcome Israel. The Middle East came under fire by terrorist attacks. Terrorist organizations were being established under their own ideologies, as in the case of the Jordanian Revolutionary Movement, formed by Nezar Hindawi. Syria later supplied this newly formed group with weapons and money. Hindawi was known for using people, to include his girlfriend, to go to locations of interest with hidden explosives. He became a lone wolf and raged his own terrorist campaigns. These campaigns and his Jordanian Movement became known as the Salafi terrorist social movement against governments. Nezar Hindawi was the mastermind of several attacks in Jordan. His movement still exists and still conducts attacks.

Regarding terrorism, Jordan doesn't tolerate it. On an international spectrum, Jordan is an important component to combat terrorism.

Because of Jordan's beliefs in Jewish and Muslim peace, they feel that violent acts of terrorism that go against religious ideologies. In fact, Jordanian officials have closed any means of money laundering in efforts to prevent terrorist organizations from collecting. Jordan is also improving their educational system to condemn terrorism. The United States has placed Jordan in a bad spot. When America invaded Iraq, refugees flooded into Jordan. Among those refugees are hidden members of terrorist groups. It was not a good thing since American diplomacy seeks Jordan's assistance on counterterrorism matters.

More on the little stuff: Canada plays a significant role in the threat of terrorism to the United States, and Canadian authorities may not be alerted to this as being true. It is important that political tenets protect the rights of others. The United States places much of this right on individuals. This type of individualism makes America unique compared to other countries like Canada, since Canada has a group approach to governance. While Canada and the United States are very different, the countries both enforced the same standards of border security until the terrorist attacks of September 11, 2001. These events spurred the two countries to conduct border security differently. United States' security is much more strict compared to that of Canada probably since there have been few terrorist attacks on Canadian soil. In truth, Canada has the largest number of terrorist groups internationally. These terrorist organizations are using Canada to aid the drug trade and raise funds for religious groups that support terrorism. Canada allowed access to terrorist groups like the IRA (Irish Republican Army) and al-Qaeda. Members of groups like this pose as refugees seeking asylum to enter Canada and then locate their organizational activities to conduct planning and logistics for attacks in America, you can Google this sentence and find information regarding this concern. It is imperative that the United States and Canada have good relations to enforce border regulations.

Here is more, Omar Khadr tossed a grenade at the end of a July 2002 firefight in Afghanistan, killing an American soldier and injuring many others. He became the youngest detainee at Guantanamo and pleaded guilty to murder and admitted to having materials that support terrorism. Khadr would serve an eight-year sentence due to the act; one year of that would be served in American custody with the remaining served in Canada. Khadr is known to have met al-Qaeda figures including Osama bin Laden and underwent terrorism training. He knowingly accepted training from al-Qaeda and intended to kill American forces members in Afghanistan. Khadr is an example of many Canadians who trained at al-Qaeda camps in Afghanistan and some still live freely in Canada.

Abdurahman Khadr testified at a court hearing at which he revealed chilling new details about Canadian terror suspects and his father's ties to Osama bin Laden's training camps. Osama bin Laden is dead, but Canada had many terrorist groups that communicated with him daily before his death. My concern with these groups is that they are living normal lives in Canada as a staging ground for a terrorist strike. Because of such chilling findings, Canada and America are part of a Joint Terrorism Task Force and assist each other at the borders.

Since the September 11, 2001 terrorist attacks on the World Trade Center, the Pentagon, and Flight 93, the president of the United States went to the international coalition for assistance in combating terrorists around the globe in areas of operations, not campaigns. Area of operations is use of military units in one country, not many, whereas campaigns are a collaborative effort of military and diplomats in many countries to achieve peaceful resolution from a specific world threat—terrorism. This was accomplished through executive order under the International Emergency Economic Powers Act, which disrupts terrorist. Now you may understand why I discussed economic financing in Chapter 17. The United Nations Security Council Resolutions already had al-Qaida Sanctions Committee1267 (1999), Security Council Resolution 1333 (2000), but enacted additional Security Council Resolution under 1390 (2002) due to President Bush's concern about global terrorism. The three resolutions together became a positive attempt toward counterterrorism efforts. The three resolutions also prove the importance of international commitment in keeping all states safe from violent terrorist actions. It was an important step for President Bush to seek assistance from the United Nations.

The United Nations also provides legal structure to all diplomatic and military action prior to execution, so clearly the United Nations resolutions mentioned above were thoroughly discussed and approved according to majority votes within the United Nations. The United Nations became concerned with weapons of mass destruction so they decided to establish 1540 (2004) which links terrorism and weapons of mass destruction (1540 Committee 2004).

> Time Line of United Nations Security Council Resolutions:
>
> "By resolutions 1267 (1999), 1333 (2000), 1390 (2002), as reiterated in resolutions 1455 (2003), 1526 (2004), 1540 (2004), 1617 (2005), 1735 (2006), 1822 (2008), 1904 (2009) and 1989 (2011). The Security Council has obliged all States to freeze without delay the funds and other financial assets or economic resources, including funds derived from property owned or controlled directly or indirectly, prevent the entry into or the transit through their territories, prevent the direct or indirect supply, sale, or transfer of arms and related material, including military and paramilitary equipment, technical advice, assistance or training related to military activities, with regard to the individuals, groups, undertakings and entities placed on the Al-Qaida Sanctions List" (United Nations website 2011).

The fact that the United Nations established 1540 with the other three resolutions gives me confidence that efforts are going in the right direction in deterring future attacks, but what about weapons of mass destruction? Today's technology is readily available to terrorist organizations. Weapons of Mass Destruction (WMD) are an emerging threat around the world. The Department of the Army's Antiterrorism Manual AR 525-13 definition of WMD is, "Any weapons or devices that are intended or have the capability of a high order of destruction and/or being used in such a manner as to destroy large numbers of people" (Army's Antiterrorism Manual AR 525-13, 2008). It can be nuclear, biological, chemical, radiological, or high-yield explosive weapons. In antiterrorism, this includes the use of very large improvised explosive devices and environmental sabotage, which is capable of destruction at the same magnitude.

These are all brief descriptions of Homeland Security concerns. There is much to learn from the topic when dealing with the prevention and mitigation of all terrorism events and natural disasters. Terrorism is not only an international issue; it is America's *Current Fight Within.* Terrorism places fear on all people, the economy, emergency services, and the military forces. I hope this book forces the reader to research the information and ideas I have presented and form their own opinions and educate others. My concern is that the American values that make our nation strong are being compromised by terrorism. When will we unite and stand strong against those that threaten the well being of our beautiful nation, the one that I love?

Judging people and world circumstances is not the best means of knowing the truth. Knowledge will touch more people and that will allow for respect to be the concrete of trust.

Semper Fidelis

Thank you for taking the time to read this book. I hope the topics pertaining to terrorism and our ability to prevent terrorism while protecting Americans and their civil liberties was of great interest. It requires all Americans to maintain the foundation of freedom.

References

104th Congress. (1995). *National highway systems designation act of 1995.* Public Law 104-59-Nov. 28, 1995. Retrieved from http://www.gpo.gov/fdsys/pkg/PLAW -104publ59/pdf/PLAW-104publ59.pdf

Abbott, B. (2005). *Checklist for state and local government attorneys to prepare for possible disaster.* Retrieved from: http://www.masgc.org/pdf/coastalstorms/checklist.pdf

Aleshinloye, S. (2011). *The 11 Most compelling 9/11 conspiracy theories.* Newsone, Associated Editor. Retrieved from http://newsone.com/newsone-original/samalesh/the-11-most-compelling-911-conspiracy-theories/

Alexander, D., and Moras, T. (2012). *Best practices in identifying terrorists during traffic stop and on call services.* Retrieved from http://www.cjimagazine.com/index2.php? option=com_content&do_pdf=1&id=176

American Psychological Association. (2011). *Factor that impact children from terrorism.* Retrieved from http://www.apa.org/about/gr/issues

Ansart, G. (n.a) *The invention of modern state terrorism during the French Revolution.* Retrieved from *docs.lib.purdue.edu/cgi/viewcontent.cgi? article=1031&context . . .*

Arlington National Cemetery Website. (2011). *William Edward Nordeen, Captain,* United States Navy. Retrieved from http://www. arlingtoncemetery.net/wenordeen.htm

Auerbach, A and Gale, W. (2009, August). *Activist fiscal policy to stabilize economic activity.* Retrieved from http://timeline.stlouisfed.org/index. cfm?p=articles&ct_id=8

Backus, Isaac, *An Appeal to the Public for Religious Liberty Against the Oppressions of the Present Day* (1773)

Baker, B. (1999). *The origins of the posse* comitatus. Retrieved from http:// www.airpower.maxwell.af.mil/airchronicles/cc/baker1.html

Balaban, V. (2005). *Posttraumatic reactions among injured children and their caregivers.* Retrieved from www.dpss.psy.unipd.it/files/docs/Moscardino/ Psychiatry_Research.pdf

Barbash, F. (2003). *U.S. cannot hold Padilla as a combatant.* Washington Post. Retrieved from http://www.washingtonpost.com/ac2/wp-dyn/ A11500-2003Dec18?language=printer

BBC. (2012). *U.S. 'foils new underwear bomb plot' by al-Qaeda in Yemen.* Retrieved from http://www.bbc.co.uk/news/world-us-canada-17985709

Best, R. (2006). *CRS issue brief for Congress.* Retrieved from http://fpc.state. gov/documents/ organization/66506.pdf

Bloy, M. (2011). *A web of English History, European History.* Retrieved from http://www.historyhome.co.uk/europe/russia1.htm

Borum, R. *(2004). Psychology of Terrorism.* Tampa: University of South Florida. Retrieved from http://worlddefensereview.com/docs/ PsychologyofTerrorism0707.pdf

Bourget, P. (2005). Hurricane Katrina: Dimensions of a major disaster. Retrieved from www.kenyoninternational.com/.../Major%20Events%20 .../Hurricane%20Katrina%20- . . .

Bruno, G. (2011). *State Sponsors*: Iran. Retrieved from http://www.cfr.org/ iran/state-sponsors-iran/p9362

Bullock, J and Coppola, D. (2009). *Introduction to homeland security*. Principles of all Hazards Response. Third Edition, Elsevier Inc.

Burns, J. (1997). *4 Americans slain in Pakistan; link to killing at C.I.A. is seen.* New York Times. Retrieved from http://www.nytimes.com/1997/11/13/ world/4-americans-slain-in-pakistan-link-to-killing-at-cia-is-seen. html?pagewant ed=all&src=pm

Burton, F., and Stewart, S. (n.a.). *Traffic stops and twarted plots*. Retrieved from http://pbtt.wordpress.com/terrorism/traffic-stops-and-thwarted-plots/

Buzzle Staff. (2006). *Large-Scale hacking discovered at State Department*. Retrieved from http://www.buzzle.com/editorials/7-12-2006-101977.asp

Bryant, C., Murphy, D., and Zirulnick, A. (2010). *Five reasons it will be hard for Yemen to 'destroy' Al Qaeda franchise*. Retrieved on May 8, 2012 from http://web.ebscohost.com/ehost/detail?vid=10&hid=19&sid=c0c0 865a-dde9-4a12-9149e028cecb60a8%40sessionmgr113&bdata=JkF1 dGhUeXBlPWlwLGNwaWQmY3VzdGlkPXM4ODU2ODk3JnNpdGU9 ZWhvc3QtbGl2ZQ%3d%3d#db=aph&AN=54864113

Carpenter, E., Felch, J., Moughty, S., Sandler, J., and Temchine, B. (2003). *Front line, the tools of counterterrorism*. Retrieved from http://www.pbs. org/wgbh/pages/frontline/shows/sleeper/tools/tools.html

CBS. (2010). *Timeline of Yemen bomb plot*. Retrieved from http://www. cbsnews.com/8301-503543_162-20021280-503543.html

Cid, D. (2008). *The Path to a counterterrorism doctrine.* MIPT: Memorial Institute for the Prevention of Terrorism. Oklahoma City, OK. Donctrine number 2008-TF-T8-K001.

Charles, P. (1999). *Are we hostages to our brains?.* Retrieved from http://www.psychplace.com/editorials/hostage/hostage2.html

Chertoff, M. (2009). *National infrastructure protection plan:* Partnering to Enhance Protection and Resiliency, Executive Summary. Retrieved from http://www.dhs.gov/xlibrary/assets/nipp_executive_summary_2009.pdf

Christopher, P. (2004). *The ethics of war and peace,* An Introduction to Legal and Moral Issues, Third Edition. Upper Saddle River, New Jersey: Pearson.

Chron. (1986). *U.S. makes case for Libya guilt using intercepted information.* Houston Chronicle Archives. Retrieved from http://www.chron.com/CDA/archives/archive.mpl/1986_231479/u-s-makes-case-for-libya-guilt-using-intercepted-i.html

Clegg, R. and Noreika, K. (2003). *Racial profiling, equal protection, and the war against terrorism.* Retrieved from http://federalistsociety.org/publication/terrorism/racialprofiling.htm

Clemson University. (N.A.). *The center for academic integrity.* Ruthland Institute for Ethics. Retrieved from http://www.academicintegrity.org/fundamental_values_project/quotes_on_responsibility.php

Collins, M. (2009, June). *Supervision spotlight on the root cause of bank failure.* Retrieved From http://www.philadelphiafed.org/bank-resources/publications/src-insights/2009/fourth-quarter/q4si2_09.cfm

CONPLAN. (2001). *Interagency domestic terrorism.* United States Government. Retrieved from http://www.fas.org/irp/threat/conplan.pdf

Cook, A. (1995). *Emergency response to domestic terrorism.* How Bureaucracies Reacted to the 1995 Oklahoma City Bombings. Retrieved from http://politicsatcontinuum.typepad.com/files/cook-emergency-response-chapter-1.pdf

Cornell Law. (2012). *Law enforcement authority of the secretary of homeland security forprotection of public property.* Retrieved from http://www.law.cornell.edu/uscode/text/40/1315

Cox, W. (2008, October). *Root causes of the financial crisis: Primer.* Retrieved from http://www.newgeography.com/content/00369-root-causes-financial-crisis-a-primer

Creamer, R., and Seat, J. (1998). *Khobar towers: the aftermath and implications for commanders.* Air War College, Maxwell Air Force Base, Alabama. Retrieved from http://www.au.af.mil/au/awc/awcgate/awc/98-082.pdf

CRS Report for Congress. (2007). *Sharing law enforcement and intelligence information.* Retrieved from http://www.fas.org/sgp/crs/intel/RL33873.pdf

Cyber-attack Techniques and Defense Mechanisms. (2002). *Investigative Research for Infrastructure Assurance Group conducted by Institute for Security Technology Studies at Dartmouth.* Retrieved from *www.ists. dartmouth.edu/library/226.pdf*

Daraisch, I. (2012). *Effects of Arab American discrimination in the context of the workplace and education system.* Retrieved from http://commons.emich.edu/cgi/viewcontent.cgi?article=1037&context=mcnair&sei-redir=1&referer=http%3A%2F%2Fwww.google.com%2Furl%3Fsa%3Dt%26rct%3Dj%26q%3Ddiscrimination%2520against%2520arabs%2520in%2520schools%2520%26source%3Dweb%26cd%3D7%26ved%3D0CGoQFjAG%26url%3Dhttp%253A%252F%252Fcommons.emich.edu%252Fcgi%252Fviewcontent.cgi%253Farticle%253D1037%2526context%253Dmcnair%26ei%3DFHzvT_KxJKa02gW4-8XCCg%26usg%3DAFQjCNG8hkrh3ujG3z0Ess_U3NL7i3ohoQ#search=%22discrimination%20against%20arabs%20schools%22

Davies, H., Plotkin, M. (2005). *Protecting your community from terrorism:* The Strategies for Local Law Enforcement Series. Police Executive Research Forum, Vol. 5, Washington D.C.

Declaration of War. (2010). *Against the Americans occupying the land of the two holy places.* A message from Usama Bin Muhammad Bin in Laden. Retrieved from: http//www.terrorismfiles.org/individuals/declaration_of_jihad1.html

Department of Homeland Security (DHS). (2012). *Department of Homeland Security budget.* Retrieved from http://www.dhs.gov/xabout/budget/dhs-budget.shtm

DHS. (2004). *Terrorist organization guide.* Retrieved from *www.nbc-links.com/ . . ./Terrorist%20Organization%20Guide.doc*

DHS. (2012). *NEXUS. U.S. customs and border security.* Retrieved from http://www.cbp.gov/linkhandler/cgov/travel/trusted_traveler/nexus_prog/nexus_facts.ctt/nexus_facts.pdf

DHS. (2003). *Nuclear incident response teams.* Retrieved from http://www.dhs.gov/xlibrary/assets/foia/mgmt_directive_9400_nuclear_incident_response_teams.pdf

DHS. (2012). *Secure borders, safe travel, legal trade.* U.S. Customs and Border Protection Fiscal Year 2009-2014 Strategic Plan. Retrieved from http://www.cbp.gov/linkhandler/cgov/about/mission/strategic_plan_09_14.ctt/strategic_plan_09_14.pdf

Digital History. (2012). *Terrorism in historical perspective.* Retrieved from http://www.digitalhistory.uh.edu/historyonline/terrorism.cfm

DoD 2000.12H. (2007). *DoD antiterrorism handbook.* Retrieved from http://www.dtic.mil/whs/directives/corres/pdf/200012p.pdf

DoD. (1985). *Lethal terrorist actions against Americans*, 1973-1985. Retrieved from http://www.dod.gov/pubs/foi/International_security_affairs/terrorism/122.pdf

DOE. (2011). *Nuclear counterterrorism program*. Retrieved from http://nnsa. energy.gov/aboutus/ourprograms/emergencyoperationscounterterrorism/ counterterrorism

DOE, NEST. (2011). *Nuclear emergency response team, NEST*. Retrieved from http://www.nv.doe.gov/library/FactSheets/NEST.pdf

DOE, AMS. (2011). *Arial measuring systems*. Retrieved from http://www. nv.doe.gov/library/FactSheets/AMS.pdf

DOE, ARG. (2011). *Accident response group*. Retrieved from http://www. nv.doe.gov/library/FactSheets/ARG.pdf

DOE, RRP. (2011). *Radiological assistance program*. Retrieved from http:// www.nv.doe.gov/library/factsheets/RAP.pdf

DOE, REACT/TS. (2011). *Radiation emergency assistance center/training site*. Retrieved from http://www.nv.doe.gov/library/FactSheets/REACTS.pdf

Department of Justice (DOJ). (2004). *The FBI's counterterrorism program since September 2001*. Retrieved from http://www.fbi.gov/statsservices/ publications/fbi_ct_911com_0404.pdf

DOJ. (2000). *Responding to terrorism victims: Oklahoma City and beyond*. Retrieved from http://www.ojp.usdoj.gov/ovc/publications/infores/ respterrorism/welcome.html

DOJ. (2005). *Terrorism 2002-2005, Federal Bureau of Investigations*. Retrieved from http://www.fbi.gov/stats-services/publications/terrorism-2002-2005/ terror02_05.pdf

DOJ. (2008). *Counterterrorism efforts*. Retrieved from http://www.justice.gov/ opa/pr/2008/September/08-nsd-807.html

Department of State. (2011). *Diplomacy in Action*. Retrieved from http://www.state.gov/r/pa/ei/rls/dos/436.htm

Department of State. (2011A). *Sponsors of Terrorism*. Retrieved from http://www.state.gov/s/ct/c14151.htm

Dewart, T., Frank, B., and Schmeidler, J. (2003). *The Impact of 9/11 on New York City's substance abuse treatment program*. Retrieved from http://www.samhsa.gov/csatdisasterrecovery/lessons/TheImpact Of911OnNYCsSaTreatment.pdf.

The Black Death. (2001). *Eyewitness to history*. Retrieved from http://www. eyewitnesstohistory.com/plague.htm*smallwarsjournal.com/documents/ gawrych.pdf*

Donahue, S., Lanzara. C., Flenton, S., and Essock, S. (2006). *Project liberty*: New York's Crisis Counseling Program Created in the Aftermath of September 11, 2001. Retrieved from http://ps.psychiatryonline.org/ article.aspx?articleid=96996

Dunbar, E. (1995). *The prejudiced personality, racism, and anti-semitism*: The PR Scale 40. Retrieved from http://edunbar.bol.ucla.edu/papers/ prejperprscale40yrs.pdf

Electronic Privacy Information Center. (2012). *United States visitor and immigrant status indicator* Technology. Retrieved from http://epic.org/ privacy/us-visit/

Ellis, J. (2007). *American creation*. Founding Brothers and His Excellency. Alfred A. Knopf Productions, New York.

Elsea, J., and Grimmett, R. (2011). *Declaration of War and Authorizations for the use of Military Forces*. Congressional Research Services. Retrieved from http://www.au.af.mil/au/awc/awcgate/crs/rl31133.pdf

Emerson, S. (2006). *Terrorist financing*. In D. Kamien (Ed.),Homeland Security Handbook (pp.207-219). The McGraw-Hill Companies.

European Commission. (2009). *Towards a comprehensive, coherent, and ethically just European counterterrorism policy.* Retrieved from http://www.transnationalterrorism.eu/tekst/publications/WP6%20Del%2013.pdf

Executive Order. (1981). *EO 12333.* The United States Intelligence Activity. Retrieved from http://www.archives.gov/federal-register/codification/executive-order/12333.html#1.13

Executive Summary. (2004). *The 9/11 commission report, final report of the national commission on terrorist attacks.* Retrieved from http://www.9-11commission.gov/report/911Report_Exec.htm

Friedman, G. (2009). *Work for Others Performed by the Department of Energy for the Department of Defense.* Retrieved from http://energy.gov/sites/prod/files/igprod/documents/IG-0829%281%29.pdf

Falk, O and Morgenstern, H. (2009) *Suicide terror, understanding and confronting the threat.* John Wiley and Sons, Inc.

Federal Bureau of Investigation. (2005). *Reports and publications, terrorism 2002-2005.* Retrieved from http://www.fbi.gov/stats-services/publications/terrorism-2002-2005

Feinstein, D. (2011). *Immigration fraud prevention act of 2011.* Retrieved from http://www.govtrack.us/congress/bills/112/s1336

FEMA. (2011). *Public communication, emergency management institute.* Retrieved from http://training.fema.gov/EMIWeb/IS/is29.asp

FEMA 592. (2007). *Robert T. Stafford disaster relief and emergency assistance act, as amended, and Related Authorities.* Retrieved from http://www.fema.gov/pdf/about/stafford_act.pdf

Find Law. (2002). *The Department of Homeland Security,* President George W. Bush, June 2002. Retrieved from findlaw.com

Forest, J. (n.a.). *The Terrorist Attacks of 9/11*: A Brief Review of Impact and Response. Retrieved from www.teachingterror.net/lectures/Ankara/ FOREST_DRAFT2.doc-

Frankena, William K. 1973. *Ethics, second edition.* Retrieved from: http:// www.ditext.com/frankena/e2.html

Ginsborg, L., Scheinin, M., and Vermeulen, M. (2011). *European and United States counterterrorism policies, the rules of the law and human rights.* Retrieved from http://www.eui.eu/Projects/GGP/Documents/ Publications/PolicyBriefs/PolicyBrief

Goldman, J. (1995). *Bomb suspect faces charges.* Indictment accused Ramzi Ahmed Yousef as the mastermind of the World Trade Center Attack and plot to blow up airliners. Retrieved from http://articles.latimes. com/1995-04-14/news/mn-54667_1_trade-center

Gomez, D. (2011). *TSA deploys on Tennessee highway.* Retrieved from http://www.tgdaily.com/opinion-features/59187-tsa-deploys-on-tennessee-highways

Goss, K. (1996). *Guide for all-hazards emergency operations planning,* FEMA. Retrieved from http://www.fema.gov/pdf/plan/slg101.pdf

Gottlied, Art. (2011). *The intelligence community, who are our spies and what do they do,* Vol 15. Retrieved from http://www.csulb.edu/colleges/chhs/ centers/olli/documents/OLLI_FALLSUN2011_REVISED.pdf

Greenemeier, L. (2012). *Screening test: are al-Qaida's airline bombing attempts becoming more sophisticated?.* A Joint CIA-Saudi Arabia intelligence coup uncovered a more effective underwear bomb designed to exploit resistance to controversial airport scans. Retrieved from http://www. scientificamerican.com/article.cfm?id=al-qaeda-underwear-bomb-2012

GSA. (2004). *Government SMART card handbook, United States General Service Administration.* Retrieved from http://www.smartcardalliance. org/resources/pdf/smartcardhandbook.pdf

Guina, R. (2008, September). *The 2008-2009 financial crisis-cause and effects*. Retrieved from http://cashmoneylife.com/2008/09/29/economic-financial-crisis-2008-causes/

Gutnick, T. (2012). *Domestic extremists seek to exploit Trayvon Martin shooting by spreading racism and hatred*. Retrieved from http://www.prnewswire.com/news-releases/adl-domestic-extremists-seek-to-exploit-trayvon-martin-shooting-by-spreading-racism-and-hatred-146872305.html

Harigel, G. (2001). *Chemical and biological weapons: use in warfare, impact on society and environment*. Retrieved from http://www.wagingpeace.org/articles/2001/11/00_harigel_cbw.htm

Henderson, N. (2002). *The Patriot Act's impact on the Government's ability to electronic surveillance of ongoing domestic communications*. Duke Law Journal. Retrieved from: http://www.law.duke.edu/shell/cite.pl?52+Duke+L.+J.+179

Herman, S. (2002). *The USA PATRIOT Act and the submajoritarian fourth amendment*. Harvard Civil Rights Journal. Retrieved from: http://www.aclu.org/files/pdfs/about/Herman,2002_usapaf.pdf

Himmat, R. (1997) *Sigmund Freud from 1856 to 1939*. Retrieved from http://www.muskingum.edu/~psych/psycweb/history/freud.htm

History of Greece. (2002). *November 17 terrorist organization*. Retrieved from http://www.ahistoryofgreece.com/press/november17terrorists.htm

Hoffman, M. (2003). *Hercules versus the methane monster*. International Health Law and Ethics. Retrieved from http://pdm.medicine.wisc.edu/Volume_18/issue_1/hoffman.pdf

Hollis, D. (2008). *Cyberwar case study: Georgia 2008*. Retrieved from *smallwarsjournal.com/blog/journal/docs-temp/639-hollis.pdf*

Hurley, B. and Thome, D. (1996) *Federal radiological monitoring and assessment center advance party phase response actions.* Retrieved from http://www.nv.doe.gov/library/publications/Environmental/anspaper.pdf

ICE. (2012). *Fact sheet: delegation of immigration authority section 287(g) immigration and nationality act.* Retrieved from http://www.ice.gov/news/library/factsheets/287g.htm

INTELECOM. (n.d.). *How pre-existing beliefs distort logical reasoning.* [Video]. Retrieved from http://www.intelecomonline.net

International Association of Chiefs of Police. (n.a) *From hometown security to homeland Security.*

IACP's Principles for a Locally Designed and Nationally Coordinated Homeland Security Strategy. Retrieved from http://www.theiacp.org/LinkClick.aspx?fileticket=78X8uKjLa0U%3D&tabid=392

Isackson, A. (2010) *Border officials see increase in passport fraud.* KPBS News. Retrieved from http://www.kpbs.org/news/2010/jun/30/border-officials-see-increase-passport-fraud/

ISLAM DENOUNCES TERRORISM. (2010). Retrieved from http://www.youtube.com/watch?v=KxG2PMuITQg

Italiano. (2009, May). *Monetary policy during the recession of 2007-2009.* Retrieved from http://understandingthemarket.com/?p=64

Jenco, L. (1996). *Hostage in Lebanon 1980's.* New York Times. Retrieved from http://www.nytimes.com/1996/07/22/us/rev-lawrence-m-jenco-61-hostage-in-lebanon-in-1980-s.html

Jenkins, H. (2012). *Wait, Who Saved the Financial System.* The Wall Street Journal. Retrieved from http://online.wsj.com/article/business_world.html

JFOB. (2007). *Joint forward operations base, JFOB.* Force Protection Handbook. Retrieved from http://www.expose-the-war-profiteers.org/archive/government/2005-2/20051100.pdf

Johnson,C.(2010). *Trafficstopthwartseco-terroristplottingtobombIBMNanotech Headquarters.* Retrieved from http://www.switched.com/2010/04/28/traffic-stop-thwarts-eco-terrorists-plotting-to-bomb-ibm-nanotec/

Joscelyn, T. (2010). *AQAP claims responsibility for cargo planes plot.* The Long War Journal. Retrieved from http://www.longwarjournal.org/archives/2010/11/aqap_claims_responsi.php

Kagan, R., and Kristol, W. (2003). *Why we went to war.* Carnegie Endowment, Publications. Retrieved from http://www.carnegieendowment.org/2003/10/20/why-we-went-to-war/89h

Kane, M. (2009, June). *Root cause of economic crisis.* Retrieved from http://washingtonindependent.com/45711/congress-passes-on-root-of-economic-crisis#

Katz, R. (n.a.) *The death of a statesmen, Aldo Moro and the unspoken terrorism.* Retrieved from http://www.theboot.it/aldo_moro_affair.htm

Kamien, D. (2006). *The McGraw-Hill Homeland Security Handbook.* New York: The McGraw-Hill Companies

Kern, M., Just, M., and Norris, P. (2003). *The lessons of framing terrorism.* In P. Norris, P. Kern, M. and Just, M. (eds), Framing Terrorism (p.2810302). London: Routledge.

Khouri, R. (2008). *Pride and shame in American politics.* Retrieved from http://proquest.umi.com/pqdweb?index=0&did=1588913761&SrchMode=2&sid=2&Fmt=3&VInst=PROD&VType=PQD&RQT=309&VName=PQD&TS=1339458999&clientId=74379

King, R. (2011). *The right news, front and center*. American's Intelligence Denial on Iran. Retrieved from http://www.ruthfullyyours.com/2011/07/20/fred-fleitz-americas-intelligence-denial-on-iran/20112.pdf

Knapp, D. (2009, March). *A handy glossary for today's economic crisis*. Retrieved from http://seekingalpha.com/article/127611-a-handy-glossary-for-today-s-economic-crisis

Kobolt, J. (1999). *Vehicle stops involving extremist group members*. Federal Bureau of Investigations, Law Enforcement Bulletin. Volume 68, Number 12.

Korematsu v. United States. (1944). *Korematsu v. United States*. Retrieved from FindLaw.com

Krekel, B. (n.a.). *Capability of the people's republic of china to conduct cyber warfare and computer network exploitation*. Retrieved from http://www.uscc.gov/researchpapers/2009/NorthropGrumman_PRC_Cyber_Paper_FINAL_Approved%20Report_16Oct2009.pdf

Kris, D. (2011). *Law enforcement as a counterterrorism tool*. Retrieved from http://www.jnslp.com/wp-content/uploads/2011/06/01_David-Kris.pdf

Kurczy, S. (2010). *Five members of al Qaeda in Yemen*. Christian Science Monitor, Article # 08827729. Retrieved from http://web.ebscohost.com/ehost/detail?vid=4&hid=122&sid=c0c0865a-dde9-4a12-9149-e028cecb60a8%40sessionmgr113&bdata=JkF1dGhUeXBlPWlwLGNwaWQmY3VzdGlkPXM4ODU2ODk3JnNpdGU9ZWhvc3QtbGl2ZQ%3d%3d#db=aph&AN=54886335

Lamm, R. (2002). *Terrorism and immigration*. The Social Contract. Retrieved from http://www.thesocialcontract.com/pdf/twelve-three/xii-3-192.pdf

Larson, R., Metzger, M., and Cahn, M. (2004). *Emergency response for homeland security*: Lessons Learned and the need for Analysis. Retrieved on http://create.usc.edu/research/50756.pdf

Leavitt, L. (1993). *The psychological effects of war and violence on children.* University of Maryland at College Park. Retrieved from http://www. questia.com/PM.qst?a=o&d=78579734

Lehrer, J. (1998). *President Clinton address.* PBS news hour. Retrieved from http://www.pbs.org/newshour/bb/middle_east/july-dec98/clinton_ 12-16.html

Lester, J. (2000). *Racism, anti-semitism and the concept of evil.* Retrieved from http://www.umass.edu/judaic/anniversaryvolume/articles/08-B1-Lester. pdf

Limmer, D. and O'Keefe, M. (2009). *Emergency care.* (11th ed.), Upper Saddle River, NJ: Prentice Hall.

Loftus, E. F. (1975). *Leading questions and the eyewitness report.* In T. F. Pettijohn, (Ed.), *Notable Selections in Psychology.* Guilford, CT: Dushkin/ McGraw-Hill.

Louisiana Office of the Governor. (2005). *Response to U.S. Senate committee on homeland security and government affairs.* Retrieved from: http:// www.agiweb.org/gap/legis109/katrina_hearings.html

Luntz, F. (2009). *Muslim women in the U.S. struggle to balance western freedoms and Islamic culture.* Fox News. Retrieved from http://www. foxnews.com/story/0,2933,511275,00.html

Maniscalco, P and Christen, H. (2011). *Homeland Security.* Principles and Practices of Terrorism Response. Jones and Bartlett Publications.

Marshall, R. (2006). *Racial steering reported*: Hewlett real estate firm accused of *racism* and *anti-Semitism* in test by advocates for fair housing. Retrieved from http://proquest.umi.com/pqdweb?index=0&did=10639 87921&SrchMode=2&sid=3&Fmt=3&VInst=PROD&VType=PQD&R QT=309&VName=PQD&TS=1339459073&clientId=74379

Masters, J. (2011). *Militant extremists in the United States.* Council on Foreign Relations. Retrieved from http://www.cfr.org/terrorist-organizations/ militant-extremists-united-states/p9236

Rubin, J. (1998). *Accountability review for Embassy bombings in Nairobi and Dareslam.* Retrieved from https://www.hsdl.org/?view&did=445269

Mathewson, J. (2011). *The psychological impact of terrorist attacks.* Lessons Learned for Future Attacks. Retrieved from http://www.au.af.mil/au/ awc/awcgate/cpc-pubs/hls_papers/mathewson.pdf

Maura, C. (2007). *TERRORISM & NEW MEDIA:* THE CYBER BATTLE SPACE: Retrieved from http://doras.dcu.ie/500/1/terrorism_new_ media_2007.pdf

McCorm, W. (2009). *State and local law enforcement:* Contributions to Terrorism Prevention. Retrieved from http://www.fbi.gov/stats-services/ publications/law-enforcement-bulletin/2009-pdfs/march09leb.pdf

Miller, L. (2004, September 17). *Bombing of Russian planes prompts more intrusive airport searches.* Associated Press, pp. A1, 12-14.

Moghadam, V. (2001). *Violence and terrorism:* Feminist Observation on Islamist Movement, State, and the International Systems. Comparative Studies of South Africa and the Middle East, Vol. XXI Nos 1&2.

Moteff, J. and Parfomak, P. (2004). *CRS Report for Congress, Critical Infrastructure and Key Assets.* Retrieved from http://www.fas.org/sgp/crs/ RL32631.pdf

Murphy, D. (2010). *AQAP bombmaker Ibrahim Hassan al-Asiri emerges as key Yemen suspect.* Retrieved from http://web.ebscohost.com/ ehost/detail?vid=6&hid=122&sid=c0c0865a-dde9-4a12-9149-e0 28cecb60a8%40sessionmgr113&bdata=JkF1dGhUeXBlPWlwL GNwaWQmY3VzdGlkPXM4ODU2ODk3JnNpdGU9ZWhvc3Q tbGl2ZQ%3d%3d#db=aph&AN=54886344

Mylroie, L. (1995). *The National Interest*. Retrieved from http://www.fas.org/irp/world/iraq/956-tni.htm

McNeill, J.; Carafano, J.; and Zuckerman, J. (2010). *Heritage Foundation*. Retrieved from http://s3.amazonaws.com/thf_media/2010/pdf/b2405_figure1_2.pdf

Nance, M. (n.a.). *Terrorist Recognition Handbook*: A Practitioner's Manual for Predicting and Identifying Terrorist Activities. Tyler and Francis Group, CRC Press.

National Counter Terrorism Calendar. (2011). *Greek domestic terrorism*. Retrieved from http://www.nctc.gov/site/groups/greek.html

National Geospatial-Intelligence Agency. (2011). Mission statement. Retrieved from https://www1.nga.mil/Pages/default.aspx

National Institute of Mental Health (2002). *Mental health and mass violence*: Evidence-Based Early Psychological Intervention for Victims/Survivors of Mass Violence. A Workshop to Reach Consensus on Best Practices. NIH Publication No. 02-5138, Washington, D.C.: U.S. Government Printing Office.

National Nuclear Security Administration Act. (NNSAA, 2004). *Title XXXII of P.L. 106-65*. Retrieved from http://www.acq.osd.mil/ncbdp/nm/nmbook/references/DOE/3.10%20National%20Nuclear%20Security%20Administration%20Act.pdf

National Reconnaissance Office. (2011). Retrieved from http://www.nro.gov/

National Response Framework. (2008). *Homeland Security*. Retrieved from http://www.fema.gov/pdf/emergency/nrf/nrf-core.pdf

National Security Division. (1998). *Terrorism in the United States*. Counterterrorism Unit. Quantico, VA: Federal Bureau of Investigations.

The National Strategy for Homeland Security, dated July 2002, *Office of Homeland Security*. Retrieved from http://www.dhs.gov/xlibrary/assets/nat_strat_hls.pdf

New York Times. (2008, September). *President George W. Bush's speech to the nation on the economic crisis*. Retrieved from http://www.nytimes.com/2008/09/25/business/worldbusiness/25iht-24textbush.16463831.html

Nettles, J. (1991). *Department of Energy, nuclear emergency search team*. Retrieved from http://www.fas.org/nuke/guide/usa/doctrine/doe/o5530_2.htm

Nixodorf, N. (2010). *Invention of the computer*. Heinz Nixdof Museums Forum. Retrieved from: http://en.hnf.de/Permanent_exhibition/1st_floor/The_invention_of_the_computer/The_invention_of_the_computer.asp

Nunez-Neto, B. (2008). *Border Security: key agencies and their missions*. CRS Report for Congress. Retrieved from http://trac.syr.edu/immigration/library/P12.pdf

Office for Victims of Crimes. (n.d.) Retrieved from United States Department of Justice http://www.ojp.usdoj.gov/ovc/publications/infores/redcross/ncj209681.pdf.

Oklahoma Department of Civil Emergency Management. (1995). *After Action Report, Alfred P. Murrah Federal Building Bombing*, 19 April 1995 in Oklahoma City, Oklahoma. Retrieved on http://www.ok.gov/OEM/documents/Bombing%20After%20Action%20Report.pdf

Or, S. (2010). *From Da'Wah to Jihad, The South African Case*. Retrieved from http://www.cms-worldwide.com/cms_south_africa_seminar.pdf

Phillips, T. (2002). *The Dozier kidnapping*: Confronting the Red Brigade. Retrieved from http://www.airpower.au.af.mil/airchronicles/cc/phillips.html

Pipes, D. (2001). *How many muslims in the United States.* New York Times. Retrieved from http://www.danielpipes.org/article/76

Professor Walter's History Lesson. (2011). *The 1920 Wall Street bombing.* Retrieved from http://www.professorwalter.com/2011/02/the-worst-terrorist-attack-in-america-up-to-that-point.html

Posttraumatic Stress Disorder. (2003). *The New York City Department of Health and Mental Hygiene.* Retrieved from http://www.nyc.gov/html/doh/downloads/ pdf/chi/chi22-1.pdf.

Proclamation No. 48 KBB 2005. (2005). *Declaring a State of Emergency.* Retrieved from http://biotech.law.lsu.edu/blaw/DOD/manual/full%20text%20documents/State%20Authorities/La.%20EOP_Supplement1b.pdf

Public Law. (2004). *Intelligence reform and terrorism prevention act of 2004.* Public Law from the 108th Congress, document number 458. Retrieved from http://www.nctc.gov/docs/irtpa.pdf

Pynoos, R., Steinberg, A., and Wraith, R. (1995). *A developmental model of childhood traumatic stress.* In: D. Cicchetti and DJ Cohen (Eds.), Manual of Developmental Psychopathology New York: John Wiley & Sons, 72-93.

Ranalli, D. (2009). *Search and seizure law of New York State.* New York: Looseleaf Law Publications.

Rogin, J. (2010). *The Top 10 Chinese Cyber-attacks.* Retrieved from http://thecable.foreignpolicy.com/posts/2010/01/22/the_top_10_chinese_cyber_attacks_that_we_know_of

Roper, R. (2003). *Reference Guide for Civil Liabilities.* Police Officers Standards Training. San Bernardino, CA: San Berardino County Sheriff's Department.

Salaam. *United States Department of State, Office of the Spokesman, Press Statement.* Retrieved from http://www.state.gov/www/regions/africa/kenya_tanzania.html

Schaffer, R. (1940). *Small Wars Manual, United States Marine Corps.* Sunflower University Press, Kansas. 1st Edition.

Schlenger, W., Caddell, J., Ebert, L., Jordan, K., Rourke, K., and Wilson, D. (2002). *Journal of the American Medical Association. Psychological reactions to terrorist's attacks.* Retrieved from: http://jama.ama-assn.org/content/288/5/581.full

Schwartz, J. (2004). *Misreading Islamist Terrorism.* Massachusetts: Blackwell Publications, Vol. 35, No. 3.

Sensenbrenner, J. (2002). *Uniting and Strengthening America by Providing Appropriate Tools Required to Intercept and Obstruct Terrorism (USA PATRIOT ACT), Act of 2001. Public Law 107-56, Bill Summary and Status of the 107th Congress H.R. 3162.* Retrieved from http://thomas.loc.gov/cgi-bin/bdquery/z?d107:H.R.3162:

Shank, Sean (2011) *"Cybersecurity*: Domestic and Legislative Issues," National Security Law Brief: Vol. 1: Iss. 1, Article 8. Retrieved on November 16, 2011 from http://digitalcommons.wcl.american.edu/nslb/vol1/iss1/8

Silke, A. (Ed.). (2003). *Terrorists, victims and society*: Psychological Perspectives on Terrorism and its Consequences. Chichester, West Sussex, UK: John Wiley & Sons, Ltd. ISBN: 9780471494621

Smilansky, S. (2010). *Terrorism, justification and illusion.* Chicago Journal. Vol. 114, 790-805. Retrieved from http://philo.haifa.ac.il/staff/smilansky/Ethics%20terrorism.pdf

Smith, W. (2001). *Terror aboard Flight 847.* The Magazine World. Retrieved from http://www.time.com/time/magazine/article/0,9171,142099,00.html

Spindlove, J.R., and Simonsen, C.E.,2010. *Terrorism Today*: The Past, The Players, Prentice Hall, Columbus, Ohio

Stewart, J. (2009). *State Department Computer Hacked*. CBS News. Retrieved on November 19, 2011 from http://www.cbsnews.com/stories/2006/07/11/national/main1794152.shtml

Stewart, S. (2010). *Al-Qaida unluck again in vargo bombing attempt*. Stratfor Press. Retrieved from http://www.stratfor.com/weekly/20101101_al_qaeda_unlucky_again_cargo_bombing_attempt

Sullivan, T.; Ellis, J.; Foster, C.; and Foster, K. (1993). *Atmospheric release advisory capability*. Real Time Modeling of Airborne Materials. Retrieved from https://narac.llnl.gov/uploads/pbamqmed.pdf

Terrorism Research. (n.a.) *International terrorism and security research, what is terrorism*. Retrieved from http://www.terrorism-research.com/

Third Jihad. (2011). *Extreme Islamic and Muslum beliefs*. Retrieved from
Part 1 - http://www.youtube.com/watch?v=ZZHnfFLZ9XU
Part 2 - http://www.youtube.com/watch?v=YbnaWpSS8Dk&feature=related
Part 3 - http://www.youtube.com/watch?v=m1d0Lx8MPtI&feature=related
Part 4 http://www.youtube.com/watch?v=QZdhKcFk5vg&feature=related

TSA. (2007). *VIPR Teams Enhance Security at Major Local Transportation Facilities*. Retrieved from http://www.tsa.gov/press/happenings/vipr_blockisland.shtm

Twlushkin, J. (1991). *The Great Revolt*. Jewish Virtual Library. Retrieved from http://www.jewishvirtuallibrary.org/jsource/Judaism/revolt.html

UNRV. (2011). *History, Hudaea-Palaestina*. Retrieved from http://www.unrv.com/provinces/judaea.php

U.S. Government Accountability Office. (2002). *Combating Terrorism.* Retrieved from http://www.gao.gov/products/GAO-03-14

USMCAT. (2007). *Antiterrorism Officers Course.* Antiterrorism and Force Protection Unit. Kansas City, MI: Marine Corps Forces Reserve.

USA Today. (2008). *Traffic Stop Part of the War of Terrorism.* Retrieved from http://www.usatoday.com/news/attack/2002/01/21/hijacker-traffic-ticket.htm

United States Court of Appeals. (2003). *For the Second District.* Retrieved from: http://news.findlaw.com/wp/docs/padilla/padrums121803opn.pdf

US Debt Clock. (2012). *The United States debt subject to limit.* Retrieved from http://www.usdebtclock.org/

U.S. House of Representatives. (2005). *Select committee to investigate the preparation for the response to hurricane Katrina.* Retrieved from: http://katrina.house.gov/

U.S. Today. (2012). *CIA thwarts new al-Qaida underwear bomb* plot. Retrieved from http://www.usatoday.com/news/washington/story/2012-05-07/al-qaeda-bomb-plot-foiled/54811054/1

United States Intelligence Community. (2009). *An Overview from the 111th Congress.* Retrieved from http://www.dni.gov/overview.pdf

Viotti, P and Kauppi, M. (2009). *International Relations and the World Politics.* Security, Economy, and Identity, Fourth Edition. Upper Saddle River, New Jersey.

Wade, C. and Tavris, C. (2000). *Psychology (6th ed.).* Upper Saddle River, NJ: Prentice Hall.

Waugh, W. (1983). *The value in violence*: Organization and Political Objectives of Terrorist Groups. Retrieved from *journals.hil.unb.ca/index.php/JCS/article/download/14600/15669*

Waters, M.; Fussell, E. (2010). *The impact of hurricane Katrina on the mental and physical health of low-income parents in New Orleans.* American Journal of Orthopsychiatry, Vol. 80, No. 2, 233-243.

West, M and Miller, P. (2001). *The rail road police, history of the rail road.* Retrieved from http://www.therailroadpolice.com/index.htm

The White House. (2011). *The Executive Branch.* Retrieved on October 15, 2011 from http://www.whitehouse.gov/our-government/executive-branch

Wiengroff, R. (n.a.). *Federal-Aid Highway Act of 1956*: Creating the Interstate System. Retrieved from http://www.fhwa.dot.gov/publications/publicroads/ 96summer/p96su10.cfm

YouTube. *1993 Bombings of the World Trade Centers.* How Investigators Located Suspects from the Vehicle Identification Number of the Rental Truck. Retrieved from http://www.youtube.com/watch?v=zhsRMIC4KXA

Yursal, A., and Arnas, F. (2010). *Six terrorist suspects caught in traffic stops.* Retrieved from http://www.thejakartaglobe.com/home/six-terrorist-suspects-caught-in-traffic-stop/368927

Zalman, A. (2011). *1988 Pan Am Flight 103 Bombing Over Lockerbie, Scotland.* About.com. Retrieved from http://terrorism.about.com/od/originshistory/p/PanAmBombing.htm

Ziegler, J. (1998). *From Beirut to Khobar Towers*: Improving the Combating Terrorism Program. Retrieved from http://www.au.af.mil/au/awc/awcgate/acsc/98-312.pdf

About the Author

Edward Ackley was born in Bridgeport, Connecticut, and raised in the town of Fairfield. Prior to his Marine Corps Career Ed was a volunteer firefighter, and participated in Law Enforcement Explorers Post 279, which was an organization under Learning for Life. He joined the Marine Corps December 14, 1994. While serving as an active service member in the Marine Corps, he experienced combat as a staff non-commissioned officer, served four tours as an embassy security guard, was bestowed the honor in becoming a drill instructor and making Marines for the future of the Marine Corps, and accepted and accomplished many opportunities. He retired from the Marine Corps officially in 2013 under permanent disability retirement's list.

Printed in the United States
By Bookmasters